The Thomas Jefferson Building as seen from the Capitol Plaza

Entrance to
the Great
Hall of the
Thomas
Jefferson
Building

Guide to
The Library
of Congress

Library of Congress
Washington 1985

Guide to The Library of Congress was written by Charles A. Goodrum and Helen W. Dalrymple, who also handled the picture research. The authors received abundant cooperation from numerous members of the staff of the Library, for which they are grateful. The following persons in the Publishing Office produced the volume: Dana J. Pratt, Director; Iris Newsom, Editor; and Johanna Craig, Production Manager. The designer was Pat Taylor, Washington, D.C.; and the printer, Stephenson, Inc., Alexandria, Virginia. The *Guide* was first published in 1982; this edition was revised and updated in 1985.

The *Guide* was produced through the Clapp Publication Fund, which was established in honor of Verner W. Clapp, Chief Assistant Librarian of Congress, upon his retirement in 1956 after a long and distinguished career in the Library.

Library of Congress Cataloging in Publication Data

Library of Congress.
  Guide to the Library of Congress.

  Includes index.
  Supt. of Docs. no.: LC 1.6/4:L61/2
  1. Library of Congress. I. Goodrum, Charles A.
  II. Dalrymple, Helen W. III. Title.
Z733.L735L48 1982   027.573   82-600095
ISBN 0-8444-0393-8   AACR2

Cover:
Dome of the Main Reading Room
Thomas Jefferson Building

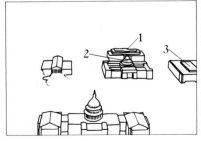

Front endpapers
Adams Building 1
Jefferson Building 2
Madison Building 3

The Library is engaged in a major restoration of the two historic buildings, the Jefferson and the Adams, so there will be periodic relocation of reading rooms. Readers are urged to ask any of the security officers in the buildings for the current location of the facility desired.

Contents

A Welcome from The Librarian of Congress

WELCOME to your Library. If you are an American, this is your library because it records and embodies, more richly than anywhere else, the history and achievements of our nation. If you are not an American, it also belongs to you because, more than any other national library, the Library of Congress brings together the recorded achievements of all mankind.

We hope that the beauty and grandeur of this place will entice you to stay awhile and become an explorer among our books, newspapers, magazines, maps, photographs, prints, manuscripts, motion picture films, and musical recordings. But simply by being here, by looking and listening, by admiring, wondering and reflecting, you help fulfill this national library. The Congress and the architects of these buildings intended here "a museum of literature, science, and art"— one of the great national monuments of any century. They hoped this Library would become "the mecca of the young giant Republic," where citizens could make their pilgrimage to our whole national past and discover our place in the civilizations of the world. The first part of this readable guide takes you into this unexcelled museum of our nation's culture and our hopes and shows how much you can learn even on a brief walking visit.

The collections and services of the Library are concisely described in the second half of this book. You will be led to what you are looking for and will be reminded of how much more there is here than you had ever expected there could be. You will find your bearings for your own sallies into the vast and enormously varied terrain of the world's knowledge. You will discover here, at your service, the world's greatest Multi-Media Encyclopedia.

The real wealth of this Library is people. The Congress, the staff who have built the Library of Congress over two centuries, the countless scholars who have found unsuspected meanings in the treasures of this place, and the millions of visitors. You help make this our national library by letting us help you recapture the American experience.

Daniel J. Boorstin

Daniel J. Boorstin
The Librarian of Congress

The Librarian of Congress, Daniel J. Boorstin, in the traditional office of the Librarians of Congress

This is
The Library of Congress —

CONGRESS'S LIBRARY. It was first created to help the senators and congressmen make the laws needed to run the country, but as it grew through the years, it became the world's largest library, and for over a century now, Congress has shared it with the nation.

The Library is approaching its two hundredth birthday. It was founded in 1800, when the government moved from New York City to the new District of Columbia, and when the Library was begun it had but one purpose: to gather the information the members needed for their day-to-day work on the floors of the Congress. But about three generations into its life, the Library took on a second responsibility: to capture the history of the American people. It set out to accumulate and store the record of the nation's life. It sought to get a better understanding of where the American people came from in "The Old Country," and it began to be recognized as the nation's memory, the place where the story of the American Experience was kept. By the time the Library reached the twentieth century, it had made *all* knowledge its province, and was trying to accumulate everything that was known by *all* cultures. It was trying to build a single treasury where the creative and questioning Americans could go to find "all the answers stored in a single place."

The combination of these three purposes has led to the superlatives that seem to cling to the Library like filings to a magnet. It *is* the largest library in the world. It *does* have more phonograph records, more manuscripts, more Stradivari violins, more flutes, more letters by George Washington, more newsreels, more cookbooks, and more writings about the North and South Poles than any other place on earth. It has 20 million books, but these represent less than a fourth of the holdings of the Library. Of the 20 million books, less than a fourth are in English, with the other three-quarters in some 470 languages (the majority of which—like Japanese, Chinese, Thai, Arabic, Hebrew, and Hindi—are in scripts that are unfamiliar to most Americans).

The library employs over five thousand staff members. About half of these acquire, process, and make the Library's materials available to the public, but the other half are occupied in the production of new materials or the provision of services quite removed from the books and documents of the Library's collections. There are some nine hun-

The Main Reading Room of the Library of Congress

dred specialists who work exclusively for the Congress providing cost projections, pro and con studies, and legislative analyses related to the routine work of the legislature. Another group provides services to the blind and the physically handicapped of the nation under a multi-million-dollar program which distributes records, tapes, and braille to those who cannot use printed materials. The Library houses the Copyright Office of the United States; it also contains the nation's largest preservation laboratory, provides computerized bibliographic data to libraries around the world, makes folk music recordings, and stages concerts, literary programs, and similar activities several steps removed from what is usually expected of a typical public or university library.

How did this unlikely institution come to be, and especially, how did it come to be the private library of the *legislature*—a situation unlike anything that exists in any other nation of the world?

A BRIEF EARLY HISTORY
The Founding Fathers brought their perception of books as working tools to their very first meeting in Philadelphia. The early representatives were lawyers and merchants and plantation owners with large personal libraries that they used in their daily work, and in 1774, when all these working bookmen convened as the Continental Congress, one of their first acts was to secure access to the volumes of the Library Company of Philadelphia. Fifteen years later when they reconvened as the first Congress of the United States they quickly obtained the use of the 4,000 volumes of the New York Society Library. In both cases the books were housed just down the hall in the same buildings where the meetings were held.

When the national government was finally moved to its permanent home in the new capital in Washington (1800), there were no literary facilities of any kind in the city, so the law that paid for the transfer from Philadelphia to the District of Columbia contained a specific instruction to create a library for the Congress to be housed in the new Capitol building. The catalog of the books purchased in the first dozen years of the institution still exists, and it is interesting to note that between 1800 and 1812 the first Librarian of Congress accumulated 3,000 volumes across a very broad, general span of interest. From the outset, the congressional library was well supplied with belles-lettres, the texts of the current English plays, poetry, and novels, as well as the law, history, and political science that would be expected. There were books on medicine and agriculture, and an amazing number of maps and atlases of the North American continent—

the latter were provided not to tell the Americans where their country was, but (according to the justifications for purchase at the time) to be able to prove borders and presence in defense of expected conflicts with England, Spain, and France which still owned and occupied the country surrounding the United States.

During the Napoleonic Wars, the United States sided with the French and in 1813 American troops burned the Parliament House and the Parliamentary Library of Canada (in present day Toronto). In 1814 a British force seeking revenge stormed into Washington and burned the White House and the Capitol, and with the Capitol it destroyed the original Library of Congress. Within a month, Thomas Jefferson, who had retired from the presidency and was living in Monticello, offered his personal library as a replacement. Jefferson had accumulated his collection during a public career of many years in this country and abroad, and the result was not only one of the largest libraries in America, but probably the broadest in scope on the continent. Congress considered Jefferson's offer in a purely political manner. New England was against buying the books (including a no from Daniel Webster), the Mid-Atlantic was mixed, but a unified vote by the South carried the measure. The Congress acquired the entire collection—paying $23,950 for its 6,487 volumes—which arrived in a single shipment of ten horse-drawn wagons brought across the tobacco roads of Virginia.

In its early years, the Library was housed in a succession of rooms in the Capitol where it was presided over by a committee on the Library with members from both Houses. The committee recognized from the outset that the Jefferson collection was a national treasure, so new materials were added constantly across the entire subject range to keep it as comprehensive and catholic as it had been when it was first created. Jefferson had organized the books, incidentally, according to a philosophical scheme of Sir Francis Bacon's in which Bacon attempted to categorize the "faculties needed to comprehend knowledge." Jefferson had modified Bacon's list into forty-four specific categories, and a century later even after the rest of the country was turning to the Dewey Decimal System, the congressional librarians remained with the forty-four-number classification scheme straight into the administration of Theodore Roosevelt.

For the first years, the Library of Congress could only be used by members of Congress and the justices of the Supreme Court. Then, as the century progressed, access was granted to the individual members of the cabinet, then the diplomatic corps, and ultimately senior members of all three branches of the government. In 1825 there was a small fire in the Library which burned some duplicate volumes (Daniel Webster was among those who helped put it out), and again in 1851 another fire broke out, this one from an overheated flue in the floor below. The second disaster destroyed two-thirds of the cumulated holdings, some thirty-five thousand volumes, including a large number of original Gilbert Stuart paintings of the revolutionary war leaders, many rare John James Audubon watercolors, and a substantial portion of the Jefferson library. Congress voted a massive appropriation to replace the books plus the construction of a large, multigalleried series of rooms across the mall side of the Capitol building. The new space was designed exclusively for the Library of Congress, and the frequent references which appear in contemporary records ("left the floor and went to the Iron Room to get proof of my assertion") refer to the cast iron shelving, spiral staircases, and metal furniture used throughout the new facilities.

By the close of the Civil War, the Library of Congress had grown to 82,000 volumes and, although occasionally a researcher from a federal agency was permitted to sit at a table and use a book, the Library was overwhelmingly intended for members of the legislature. Recall that there were no congressional office buildings other than the Capitol itself for the first hundred years, and therefore the entire legislative branch was simply "down the hall" from its Library and it was used accordingly.

FROM CONGRESSIONAL LIBRARY TO NATIONAL LIBRARY

The "Congress-only" years lasted until the arrival of Librarian of Congress Ainsworth Rand Spofford who was appointed by President Lincoln in 1864. Spofford was eager to give the legislators the finest possible library service, but he was convinced that, in order to do this, he needed a much larger collection of books. He thus dedicated himself to bring in "oceans of books and rivers of information," and set out to gather the printed word in quantity for his employers.

He began by directing the copyright channels onto the Library's shelves. There had been copyright legislation on the books from the founding of the republic but for the previous eighty years it had been casually observed at best. By the time Librarian Spofford became interested, a book or picture was given copyright protection by filing a claim with the clerk of the nearest district court. An author or artist would give the clerk a dollar to keep, and then would send a copy of the published work to whatever agency was currently burdened with the responsibility. By 1869 registration had been passed from the Department of State to the Patent Office in the Department of Interior—where the task was cordially resented by all. Librarian Spofford perceived the copyright device as a marvelous means of getting free books for the Library of Congress so, by pressing his legislative patrons, in 1870 he got the copyright law changed. The new version declared that anyone claiming a copyright on any book, map, chart, dramatic or musical composition, engraving, cut, print, or photograph or negative thereof must send two copies to the Librarian within ten days of its publication. Sanctions were decreed for violations, and the move was enormously successful. In the first twenty-five years it brought 371,636 books to the Library, 257,153 magazines, 289,617 pieces of music, 73,817 photographs, 95,249 prints, and 48,048 maps.

At the same time Spofford was collecting all copyright receipts, he entered into an agreement with the Secretary of the Smithsonian Institution to house in the Library of Congress its ever-growing collection of American scientific materials and foreign exchange documents. The latter were pouring in from around the world as the result of the free distribution of Smithsonian studies to any literate country abroad. Spofford got a law passed that gave him a hundred free copies of the *Congressional Record* and the statutes of the United States, and with these he established exchange agreements with *all* foreign countries who had diplomatic relations with the United States. This produced the thousands of gazettes, Hansards, and acts of law which today give the Library the largest and most complete collection of government documentation in the world.

Each of these devices produced tens of thousands of pieces every month, automatically and free, and thus freed Spofford for his next target: recovering those parts of the nation's publishing he had missed before coming to office. To achieve this, he began buying complete private collections of historical materials, medical records, political manuscripts, eighteenth-century newspapers, and libraries of missionaries and retired foreign service officers.

The results of all these efforts could have been foreseen. First, he ran out of room. He had filled up all the space given him in the "Library Rooms" almost at once. He then filled the attics of the Capitol, then the hallways, and was encroaching on committee space when his goodwill ran out. Second, in order to get the Smithsonian library and exchange materials, he had to promise to let scholars and the general public have access to them, and he had to promise to keep his reading rooms open seven days a week, from nine to nine. The result was that he quickly ran out of tables, chairs, and space for his patrons. Third, the copyright deposits had to be acknowledged for legal purposes, the fees coming in had to be accounted for and turned over to the Treasury, and the resulting paperwork absorbed all the time of his catalogers and librarians. By the mid 1870s he had abandoned cataloging, ceased to shelve books in any consistent order, and given up keeping sequential copies of magazines, newspapers, and federal documents together. He began to plead for a separate library building where he could make the collections available to the scholarly world.

THE BUILDING

Librarian Spofford recognized his growing difficulties as early as 1871. For a brief time he was torn between the two souls of the Library. As Congress's library, it needed to be in the Capitol building, within walking distance of the Senate and House floors. As the nation's library, it needed a separate building where the collection could expand endlessly, and where the nation's scholars could be served with efficiency. He quickly committed himself to the latter cause, and by 1873 the Congress had agreed to give up its within-arm's-reach relationship and give him a building solely for the Library of Congress. There is reason to believe that the legislation was passed less to gratify Librarian Spofford than to reclaim the halls, attics, and committee rooms of the Capitol for legislative business.

In the routine manner for major public buildings of the time, a competition was declared. Spofford laid out the specifications which added up to a businesslike, no-nonsense shell with a central reading room, peripheral work and special collection areas, and a book stack to hold 2.5 million volumes, which he believed would satisfy the Library's needs until 1975. (In fact, by 1975 the Library was to own 18 million volumes, not counting the nonbook materials.) The original building was to be essentially plain on the inside, but the exterior was to have such character as to make it a fitting companion to the Capitol across the street. The winner of the competition was to get $1,500, second prize was $1,000, $500 was the third, and another $1,000 was to be divided among the next seven competitors.

Ultimately, twenty-eight designs were submitted and the winner was an Italian Renaissance-style facade conceived by two Washington architects who teamed up for the contest, John L. Smithmeyer and Paul J. Pelz.

Although the Italian design may have won first prize, the Joint Committee on the Library did not like it and promptly announced a second competition. Another forty-one designs were submitted, this time involving a classic Greek facade that looked like a mirror image of the Capitol portico; another architect drew wings on the Capitol like the enfolding galleries of St. Peter's; and Smithmeyer and Pelz submitted additional drawings. The Joint Committee kept changing the rules. Sometimes the building was to face the Capitol directly, sometimes it was to lie near where the Botanic Garden now is, at other times it was to be located on Judiciary Square toward the White House. The size and theme kept shifting and ultimately Smithmeyer and Pelz had tried a Victorian Gothic library, others in French, German, and "Modern" Renaissance styles, and finally an oversized paraphrase in the Romanesque. At long last, in 1885 the Joint Committee settled on a modified version of the Smithmeyer and Pelz design that had won the original prize in 1873.

A Temple of the Arts

Between 1873 and 1885, however, the attitude toward the building had changed in everyone's mind. It was originally perceived as a functional library, but by the time the excavation was begun it was seen as a "showplace." The architects declared that "the National Library of the United States" should be "more a museum of literature, science, and art, than strictly taken as a collection of books." They believed that each American would want to visit it in his lifetime, making it "the mecca of the young giant Republic." By the time the building was actually built the nation had moved from post-Civil War recovery to a high level of assertive nationalism, and there was general agreement that culture and art were the most valid indexes of a civilization. The Library was therefore embraced as coming proof of how cultured the American people were.

Construction

The site was finally settled on and the excavation was begun in 1886. The hole was completed by August 1887, but the architects became embroiled in an argument with one of the contractors that brought everything to a full stop. Six months went by while Smithmeyer con-

The Thomas Jefferson Building takes shape —status of construction as seen from the Capitol on ember 25, 1892.

ducted 615 tests on various kinds of cement. The Congress became so frustrated that it demanded an investigation which took from May to September 1888 and ended with firing Smithmeyer and handing the project over to Brigadier General Thomas Lincoln Casey (chief of the Army Engineers) and a civil engineer by the name of Bernard Richardson Green. These two in fact created the building we now know, bringing it in under budget and ahead of the legislated deadline.

The Great Hall of the Thomas Jefferson Building

The building was constructed with a complicated combination of steel and prefabricated cast iron parts; the inner arches were brick surrounded by fifteen kinds of marble on the interior and the complete edifice was encased in New Hampshire granite on the outside. There was to be no flame within the building; it was to be heated by furnaces almost a mile away and the hot air blown through brick tunnels under the neighboring streets. The tunnels, in turn, led into flues going up inside the Library walls, and the building was thus heated by forced hot air coming out of grills in the sides of the window wells. The window frames themselves were cast iron formed to look like chiseled marble to match the ornamentations of the rooms surrounding them.

Decoration of the Building

Indeed it was the decoration of the building that not only made it the wonder of its time, but has given it immortality as the prime example of "American Renaissance" architecture existing in our own genera-

On-site carving studios were set up in unfinished rooms throughout the Thomas Jefferson Building.

tion. Late in the nineteenth century, Bernard Berenson declared that "because of our faith in science and the power of work [we] are instinctively in sympathy with the Renaissance." The Library was deliberately designed to demonstrate America's love of learning, science, work, and culture. Each square foot of the spectacular ornamentation of the walls was planned by Green or General Casey's son, Edward Pearce Casey. Over fifteen hundred fully developed architectural drawings were prepared in the architects' offices. Green turned to the leading artistic associations and asked, "Who are

Ornamental ceiling in the hall outside the Library's original House of Representatives Reading Room in the Thomas Jefferson Building

the outstanding practitioners of your craft?" The nominees were then offered crisp, businesslike contracts—such as, "$5,000 for a full figure, 24 months delivery"—and ultimately fifty-two leading American artists were commissioned and descended on the building en masse. In one of the hundreds of articles about the building that appeared as it grew and was decorated, *Century* magazine noted, "the artists like the workmen, were in overalls, and the atmosphere of the place impregnated with the spirit of art and labor. It was something as it must have been in Florence or Venice in the Renaissance."

One of the most unusual aspects of the decoration is that in spite of the breathless complexity in detail, the total effect melds together so beautifully. The murals run from modern interpretations of Pompeian wall paintings (see the figures of Justice and Fortitude floating in the air of the second floor gallery dressed in togas held together with garters, straps, and leather-stripped armor) to the severely modern women (F. W. Benson's Seasons and Graces on the second floor ceiling) who could have been lifted off a magazine cover or a present-day cigarette advertisement. Note how the floor mosaics, most of them crafted in Italy and sent back pasted face down on brown paper sheets, reflect the complicated allegorical paintings on the overhead vaults—neither artist ever having seen the other's product when it was created.

There are over a hundred mural paintings and hundreds of square yards of ornamental vines, cornucopias, ribbons, and garlands inside the building, plus forty-two granite sculptures and yards of bas-reliefs on the outside. Each theme symbolizes some aspect of civilization. There are myths and legends from classical literature, the various seasons of nature, the ages of man, and ways of transmitting learning and knowledge. The civilizing institutions of the family, government, religion, and art are celebrated, with the intervening spaces filled with uplifting quotations from the great minds of all the world's cultures.

The Sculptures

Twenty sculptors were commissioned, many to do several different pieces in different parts of the building. Most of the men had known each other on previous World's Fair assignments and went on from the Library experience to do some of our most famous national symbols. The Library's statues of History holding a backward-looking mirror (in the Main Reading Room) and Herodotus striding with a staff (bronze on the Main Reading Room upper balustrade) were modelled by Daniel Chester French who also gave the nation the im-

age of the Minute Man at Concord, Columbia University's "Alma Mater," and the great seated Lincoln of the Lincoln Memorial in Washington. The Main Reading Room's "Art" was designed by Augustus Saint-Gaudens of the Metropolitan Museum's "The Puritan" and the Adams Memorial (popularly known as "Grief") fame. Frederick MacMonnies did the three-ton bronze door, "The Art of Printing," at the entrance to the Library, as well as the Nathan Hale Statue in City Hall Park in New York City. The Main Reading Room rotunda's "Poetry" was done by John Q. A. Ward, who did the statue of George Washington in Wall Street and was the president of the National Sculpture Society for many years.

The artistic proliferation was directed with military precision. General Casey and Engineer Green would consult with Librarian Spofford on figures and images. Spofford would provide the names and symbols, and the contractors would tell the artist what he was to provide and where. How he did it was up to the artist; what he did was rigorously supervised by the builders. One of Casey's letters to Paul Wayland Bartlett is typical: "there is no improvement to be suggested concerning the figure of *Law,* but I want to say regarding *Columbus* that, while it is very good and has a good deal of character the figure is so broad or *large round,* and the coat so short comparatively as to seem a little droll, a tendency however that you certainly will have no difficulty in correcting. How soon may we expect to receive your sketch of *Michelangelo?"* Monthly state-of-the-work bulletins were sent to all participating artists like military campaign reports.

The portico of the building facing the Capitol was to be dominated by the portrait statues of the nine most important writers in Western civilization. Each sits in front of a five-foot, dark circular window to make the bust project in sharp relief. The nine great figures are Demosthenes, Emerson, Irving, Goethe, Macaulay, Hawthorne, Scott, and Dante, with Benjamin Franklin positioned in the dramatic center. How were these particular figures selected? They were simply the personal favorites of Librarian Spofford, who thought it was hopeless to try to get a committee to make such a subjective choice.

Similarly, the four faces of the building are dominated by thirty-three "ethnological heads." These are carved into the keystones of each of the major, arched windows; the spaces were originally planned to contain the traditional Gorgon head or Janus of Renaissance buildings. Engineer Green, however, had seen a number of life-size models of distant races in the Smithsonian Institution's Department of Ethnology. Green consulted with the supervisor of the department about the possibility of using a series of "all the races of the world" around the building; two local sculptors did the Australian and Japanese heads as trial runs; Green liked the way they looked and ordered thirty-one more.

The eleven-foot statues at the top of the Main Reading Room columns symbolize "the eight characteristic features of civilized life and thought." Each column becomes a cumulative statement with the white, togaed woman as the centerpiece, and a tablet over her head declaring the theme which she represents. John Flanagan's "Commerce" holds a Yankee schooner in her right hand and in her left a steam locomotive; St. Gaudens's "Art" is a nude holding a model of the Parthenon before her with a sculptor's mallet and a painter's pallette and brushes hung in the bush beside her feet. An appropriate inscription crowns each figure, the quotations having been selected by President Eliot of Harvard University. (Eliot had chosen "memorable sentences" which had been carved around the New York Post Office and, following his selections for the Library, went on to determine the extensive inscriptions chiselled into the Washington Union Station facade.) "Commerce" is celebrated with the quotation, "We taste the spices of Arabia yet never feel the scorching sun which brings them forth," and "Art" carries a tablet with these words by James Russell Lowell, "As one lamp lights another, nor grows less, So nobleness enkindleth nobleness." Finally, on either side of the classical figures, two bronze, life-size statues stand on the highest of the Main Reading Room galleries. These, too, celebrate the associated civilizing characteristic. On either side of "Commerce," for example, the bronze figures of Robert Fulton and Christopher Columbus overlook the readers; "Art" is flanked by Michelangelo and Beethoven. While such a proliferation of detail might be expected to produce a confusion of distracting elements, instead the ornamentation flows together to produce a visual crescendo of effects as everything mounts to the great rotunda overhead.

The Paintings

There are 112 major "pieces of composition" in the decoration of the walls, as well as hundreds of "designs and inscriptions." The four corner pavilions on the second floor are the most complicated and dramatic and for these the artists were paid $8,000 apiece; simple tympana at the ends of each room brought $4,000 each.

The murals throughout the building are painted on canvas (they are not wet plaster frescoes), but the majority were painted in place. This resulted in complicated scaffolding being erected throughout

"Melpomene" and "Calliope," the Greek muses of tragedy and epic poetry

the building. When the rotunda of the Main Reading Room was decorated, a wheeled structure was built that was 120 feet high and an eighth of the room wide; this was pivoted around the room as the painters and plasterers worked. The building had its share of tragedies. A seventeen-year-old helper fell through a materials lift hole in the rotunda and was killed, and the master mason of the work had his right hand crushed when the second portico column at the left of the entrance broke loose from its rigging and dropped directly onto the plinth below.

Outstanding Features

The artists were permitted to express their assignments in whatever style they saw fit, always subject to the approval of General Casey and Engineer Green. Every major element of the Library has a story behind it, either of its theme or how it came to be made, but space does not permit such a telling here. *A Handbook of the New Library of Congress in Washington* by Herbert Small, may be purchased at the Library (current edition, 1982). Profusely illustrated with recent pictures, many in color, it accounts for each artistic element. For the present visitor with limited time, a description follows of four representative units that have held the attention of respected critics for the past century.

The Neptune Fountain   The Court of Neptune Fountain sits at street level in the front of the building. The fountain contains a dozen bronze figures scattered among rocks and sea grottoes, and was deliberately designed to capture the feel of the fountains of Rome without copying any specific model. The figures were created by Roland Hin-

18

The coffered Main Reading Room dome is ornamented with sea shells, griffins, cherubs, garlands, and the panoply of classic architectural designs.

ton Perry. Neptune, the god of the sea, sits nude on the central rocks, cast in classic size as well as mode. If he were to stand, he would be twelve feet high. Neptune is flanked by two figures of his son, Triton, who is spraying jets of water from two conch shells. (Triton is traditionally credited with making the sound of the sea, and it is his trumpet which is heard in a sea shell held to one's ear.) The women on either side are described as sea nymphs astride rearing sea horses. Water is sprayed back and forth across the fifty-foot basin from the mouths of sea snakes, two turtles, and a pair of over-sized frogs. The fountain is a delight of coursing water in the heat of the summer, but oddly enough is even more attractive in the sleet and snow of winter when the frozen water reinforces the curves and planes of the smooth bronze.

Mosaics and Marble   Within the building the viewer is swept up in the decorations, the vaulted spaces, and above all else, the color. The latter comes not only from the ornamentation of the artists, but the astonishing use of marble in the floors, stairs, walls, and even the ceilings. In every public space there will be one or more of the polished sheets. The white of the Great Hall is Italian marble. The brown bands in which the brass sun and zodiacal signs are set in the floor are from Tennessee, as are the bases of the piers in the Main Reading Room. The dark red blocks in the floor designs are from France. The blue marbles in the east corridor are from Vermont, and the forty-four-foot

Columns and mosaics in the Great Hall show some of the many varieties of marble used throughout the Thomas Jefferson Building.

"The Sciences," a mural by Kenyon Cox in the Thomas Jefferson Building

piers of the Main Reading Room are mottled, dusky red from Numidia in North Africa. The eight Numidian columns are tied together by arcaded screens of Siennese marble running from yellow through cream and topaz sheets to their accents of jet black veining.

The mosaics that appear everywhere were produced by an unusual technique. In each case, the "cartoon" and the color were determined by the individual artist, who drew the picture or design, full size, on art paper. These paper sheets were then sent to Italy where they were backed by layers of heavier paper and laid out on the floors of the mosaicists' lofts. The paper was then covered with sticky glue and the cartoons filled in, a tiny piece at a time, from marble chips in the manner of present "painting by numbers." When the complete cartoons were covered, the sheets were boxed and returned to the Library where they were placed face down in wet cement. When the cement had hardened, the paper backing was scrubbed off and the marble ground smooth with sandstone.

The same technique was used for the overhead mosaics seen at the heads of the staircases—except here the chips or tessera were simply pounded into the cement or stucco of the ceilings, the paper removed, and the rough base left unpolished to provide a pleasing texture.

The mural of Minerva which dominates the central stairs of the second floor (indeed of the whole front pavilion) is a mosaic by Elihu Vedder. Minerva was chosen as the appropriate patroness of the Library because she was the Roman goddess of wisdom and protectress of arts and industries. Legend reports she burst fully armed from the brow of Jupiter, shrieking a terrible battle cry; she is pictured here still armored but carrying her spear in repose. The mosaic is saturated with symbolism from the laurel vine around the border to the "clouds of disaster and discouragement . . . rolled away and about to disappear, while the sun of reappearing prosperity sends its rays into every quarter of the land." The painter carefully explained that although her shield and helmet have been placed on the ground before the little statue of Victory, she still holds the spear "showing that she never relaxes her vigilance against the enemies of the country she protects." The scroll in her left hand lists the "departments of learning" important to a civilized land including law, statistics, mechanics, biography, and arbitration. Her owl of wisdom sits on a balustrade which in turn overlooks olive trees symbolizing peace. Generations of children visiting the Library have been intrigued with the optical illusion that, no matter how far to the right or left the viewer stands on the upper galleries, Minerva's bare feet appear to be pointed directly at the observer.

One of the most unusual features of the Library's ornamentation is the "cascade of marble babies" that runs down the railings on either side of the Great Hall. There are twenty-six of them, each two to three feet high and, of course, symbolizing some uplifting thought. In the center of the staircases are two globes of the earth with a representative baby sitting by the appropriate continent. "Europe" is dressed in a toga with a lyre, a book, and a Doric column beside him representing Music, Literature, and Architecture or, as the sculptor explained, "the preeminence of the Caucasian races in the arts of civilization generally." The "Mongolian" opposite him is dressed in silk robes with a dragon-shaped porcelain jar behind him representing "the admirable ceramic art of China and Japan." On the opposite stair, a baby wearing a feather headdress personifies America, while a war club and claw necklace identify Africa. The cultural nationalism of the time is awesome in retrospect.

The remaining twenty-two children rest on the bannisters linked together with heavy festoons and ending at the base with a stork. Each child represents an occupation. The young hunter with a gun holds up a rabbit by the ears; an infant chemist has a blowpipe; an entomologist chases a butterfly; a miniature physician is grinding drugs in a mortar; and "an infant Bacchanalian" in a panther skin holds a wine glass in his hand. The modelling makes the marble look plastic, and the astonishing care lavished on the details of the sculpture gives us a design that would be unusual anywhere and is doubly unexpected in a library.

The Collar of the Dome   The Main Reading Room is dominated by its magnificent dome, 125 feet high and 100 feet wide. At the crown is a "lantern" which adds another 35 feet to the height and both admits light and permits a final decoration, in this case a mural of "Human Understanding." But around the base of the lantern is a collar, designed and painted by Edwin Howland Blashfield; it is considered by many critics to be the prime embellishment of the Library.

The design consists of twelve winged figures, each representing a country and with it that nation's contribution to the development of our civilization. The figures are huge, each over ten feet high, and both their symbolism and modern antecedents are noteworthy. The countries of the "epochs" are: Egypt giving us written records; Judea, religion; Greece contributing philosophy; Rome, administration; Islam, physics; the Middle Ages bestowing the modern languages; Italy, the fine arts; Germany, the art of printing; Spain, discovery; England, literature, France, freedom or emancipation; and America, science.

The symbolism of the figures goes beyond the broad philosophical concepts into details of dress and artifacts. Egypt not only has rolls of papyrus, but holds a Tau, the earliest symbol of a life after death. Judea is shown praying to Jehovah beside a pillar engraved with the Hebrew characters for the command, "Thou shalt love thy neighbor as thyself." Italy has a statue of Michelangelo's "David" and a Cremonan violin. The book in England's lap is a facsimile of the title page of the first edition of *A Midsummer Night's Dream*, while America sits on top of an electric dynamo.

A further step in the characterizations leads us to the models of the figures. England has the face of the actress Ellen Terry, much admired by the painter. Italy is a young sculptor from New York, a Miss Amy Rose. Spain is modelled after Blashfield's wife; the American Electrician is a portrait of a young Abraham Lincoln; and the profile of "Gutenberg" standing by the German press is Brigadier General Casey, the man from whom Blashfield received his contract for the commission.

Completion

The building was finished in 1897, the books moved out of the Capitol in shelf-length wooden boxes throughout the summer, and the museum-library was opened to the public on November 1. It was an enormous success. Half a million visitors came in the first eleven months of 1898, and newspaper and magazine articles on the Library continued to appear well into the new century. The Chairman of the Joint Committee on the Library rejoiced that it was better than anything in France or England, and as Herbert Small summarized in 1901, "America is justly proud of this gorgeous and palatial monument to its National sympathy and appreciation of Literature, Science, and Art. It has been designed and executed entirely by American art and American labor [and is] a fitting temple for the great thoughts of generations past, present, and to be."

The Library in the Twentieth Century

The new Library was headed by two vigorous Librarians, who moved it steadily from being a passive collection of books-to-be-consulted, to an active, productive institution whose activities were to influence and inspire the national cultural community.

The first Librarian in the new building was a newspaperman and a friend of General Grant's, one John Russell Young. Although Young had had no library experience, he set up organizational units which have worked with efficiency into our own time. Similarly, with astonishing speed he devised programs that changed the Library from essentially an acquisitions operation into an efficient processing factory that got control of its materials and made them quickly useful.

Young was followed by Herbert Putnam, of the publishing family and previously the head of the Boston Public Library, and he was destined to be the Librarian of Congress for forty years. While Librarian Spofford had collected the materials, and Young had organized them, Putnam *used* them. He took the Library of Congress directly into the national library scene and made its holdings known and available to the smallest community library in the most distant part of the country. The ubiquitous *printed* library card stemmed from his idea of cataloging books as quickly as the Library of Congress received them via copyright deposit or exchange, and then selling the resulting catalog cards at cost to local libraries, so the smaller institutions would be spared the expense of doing the same work themselves when they bought the same book. This program became so popular that at its height the Library was selling 87 million cards a year to American and other libraries from Tokyo to the Vatican.

Putnam organized the Library's services to the blind, designing programs that at first loaned out brailled books, then later provided phonograph records with special machines for handicapped people. (The now-familiar 33⅓ rpm record was invented for Putnam's purpose and was used in Library of Congress "talking books" for fourteen years before the commercial world embraced it.) This Library of Congress program continues to open word windows for hundreds of thousands of users around the nation.

Putnam distributed endless bibliographies so that scholars working in specialized fields could know what materials related to their special disciplines were accumulating along the interminable shelves.

About 1912, both Putnam and the Congress became concerned about the distance that was widening between the Library and its employer. Adding to the damages wrought by the geographical separation, was the frustration over "legislative reference bureaus" which were proliferating at the state government level but had no equivalent at the federal. The idea had been invented by the Wisconsin State government and involved the creation of a skilled team of librarians, economists, political scientists, and statisticians who were attached directly to the legislature to respond to hourly inquiries that arose in the legislative process. They were the legislature's own, with no link to the governor. Congress wanted the same thing for itself, with no link to the president. Under instruction, Putnam designed such a unit for the Library of Congress, and in 1914 the federal Legislative Reference Service was begun. It started as a bibliographic unit "to prepare such indexes, digests, and compilations of law as may be required for Congress," but quickly became a specialized reference unit for information transfer, and ultimately the analytical, policy-centered research service that will be described below (p. 37).

GIFTS AND BENEFACTORS
OF THE LIBRARY

From Librarian Spofford's time on, the great jewels of the Library have come from individual Americans who have given either money or private treasures to the Library to be shared with the American people. Traditionally, the routine publications of the world have come in through the copyright and the exchange programs, but the special, unique pieces have come as private gifts. Some of the most spectacular came during Putnam's time; the decade of the twenties is representative: Elizabeth Sprague Coolidge (who had become famous as the patron of the Berkshire Music Festivals) gave the Library a 500-seat auditorium specially designed for the performance of chamber music. This was built in 1925 in one of the Library's empty inner courts, and Gertrude Clarke Whittall soon gave a pavilion to house the Stradivarius violins, viola, and cello she also donated so that free concerts might be given in the Coolidge hall. (Fritz Kreisler later gave his famous Guarnerius violin to add to the collection.) The American artist Joseph Pennell presented the Library with the most complete collection of James McNeill Whistler drawings and letters in existence. Robert Todd Lincoln, son of Abraham Lincoln, gave the Library the nation's largest collection of the president's papers. The Mathew Brady collection of Civil War photographs were received at this time. John D. Rockefeller gave the Library nearly a million dol-

The bronze doors of the Rare Book and Special Collections Reading Room carry the names or marks of great printers from Fust and Schoeffer to William Morris.

Tradition, Writing, and Printing are depicted on the bronze doors to the Thomas Jefferson Building.

lars to photograph source materials relating to American history in foreign archives. A group of private individuals provided enough money to establish the American folk song project; recording teams spread throughout the country to capture ballads in jails, remote mountain communities, and Indian pueblos where the music was "endangered by the spread of the radio and phonograph, which are diverting the attention of the people from their old heritage." The Guggenheim family endowed a chair of aeronautics and underwrote the Library's effort to acquire manuscripts, personal papers, and printed materials related to the discovery of flight in America.

Occasionally, during Putnam's time, such startling private collections would come on the market that the Librarian would ask Congress's permission to purchase them as special acquisitions. Putnam bought a collection of 80,000 volumes of Russian literature from a book collector in Siberia which—after it was moved across Russia in a special train and shipped to Washington in great wooden crates— along with its previous acquisitions made the Library the largest holder of Russian research material outside of the Soviet Union. In 1930, the Otto H. F. Vollbehr collection was offered for sale, and Putnam requested a million and a half dollars to purchase this unexcelled collection of incunabula. It included over three-thousand fifteenth-century books, among which was one of the three perfect vellum copies of the Gutenberg Bible in existence. Congress made the money available with minimal delay, and when Putnam expressed his gratitude to a member, the congressman explained the reason for his support, "Mr. Putnam, we are a young country. We have no monuments. If we know where they are and can be got we ought to get 'em."

Putnam believed that not only should the Library continue to expand and enrich its collections, it should bring in nationally recognized scholars in the various fields to interpret and make more useful the materials the Library held. From this came special collections, specially endowed chairs, bibliographic publications, and compilations of unique Library of Congress materials. It published the now-famous *Guide to the Diplomatic History of the United States,* compiled the 1,115-page *Documents Illustrative of the Formation of the Union of the United States,* and produced similar titles.

The figures that adorn the bronze doors to the John Adams Building are credited with giving the art of writing to their people since ancient times.

THE SECOND BUILDING OF THE LIBRARY OF CONGRESS

Librarian Spofford had believed that his new library building would provide the space his collections and programs would need until

1975. Instead, Librarian Putnam ran out of room in the late 1920s. He made a convincing case for a second building and Congress authorized it in 1930. By the time construction began in 1935, the Folger Shakespeare Library had been completed and opened in the block to the east of the Library, and the Supreme Court had been completed to the north. The second building (then called "The Annex," now the John Adams Building) was designed primarily as a storage book stack. Its central core was built to hold twice as many volumes as the original library could; and while the annex had work rooms surrounding the stack area, it was primarily intended for Library acquisition and cataloging specialists. The only spaces expected to be used by the public were two large reading rooms on the top floor and the study carrels surrounding them.

The second building was designed at the height of the art deco period, and although far less ornamented than the Renaissance-style original building, it has aged gracefully and has proved to be an excellent example of its architectural period. Its two public areas, the fifth floor reading rooms, are dominated by four 72-foot long murals

Wrought iron gates from the Whittall Pavilion carrying the violin motif of the Stradivari Collection

running the length of the two rooms on either side. The northern room carries near-life-size paintings of all of Chaucer's Canterbury pilgrims. The thirty-two figures are on horseback and appear to be walking leisurely along a Kentish road in the order of their stories. Chaucer himself has his back to the viewer, as he rides between the Doctor of Physic and the Lawyer. The lunette on the south recreates the English countryside described in the Prologue, "Whan that Aprille with his shoures soote . . ."

The reading room to the south is surrounded by Ezra Winter's murals dedicated to Thomas Jefferson. The side panels contain quotations from Jefferson's writings which demonstrate the breadth of his interests and his philosophy. The northern lunette here is a portrait of Jefferson with his design for Monticello in the background. The two reading rooms are in a comfortable scale with handsome bronze lamps forming a part of the architectural design; although fitted into a much smaller space, the rooms in fact seat over twice as many readers (480 compared to 196) as the great reading room under the rotunda in the original building.

FROM WORLD WAR II
TO THE PRESENT

The Library's recent years have been devoted to major breakthroughs in at least three areas of its responsibilities.

The first relates to its role as the central pivot point of American scholarship. During the 1960s, Congress gave its library the responsibility for acquiring "*all* library materials currently published *throughout the world* which are of value to scholarship." Once the materials were in the Library's hands, it was to catalog them promptly and distribute the bibliographic information to the American research community so that scholars could know what information was available and how it related to their own work. From this came an enormous increase in the Library of Congress receipts (it now processes over 1.5 million items a year), which stimulated a sharp need to disseminate the bibliographic information quickly. The increased receipts came from on-site Library of Congress installations opened in New Delhi, Jakarta, Nairobi, Rio de Janeiro, Cairo, Tokyo, and the major European publishing centers. The need for more efficient cataloging dissemination led first to greater catalog card production and more recently to the invention of a basic computerized cataloging format which is now distributed by weekly digital tapes to tens of thousands of American, British, and Canadian libraries through national and regional computer facilities.

A second major development was the shift of the Legislative Reference Service (which specialized in the location and transfer of library materials relating to national issues) to the Congressional Research Service filled with specialists in a hundred fields, who analyze issues for the Congress, weighing policy alternatives, projecting probable costs and advantages, and estimating the damage the alternatives might do.

Third, while holding the present level of acquiring and processing *books,* the Library recognized that the future of data collection and preservation lies equally in the nonbook formats—videodiscs; computerized, digital memory; microforms, such as, microfiche, microfilm, microcard; and motion pictures and television tape, and recorded sound in its many formats. The Library recognizes that it is the facts and images and sounds of America that form its history and its stored knowledge, and not the devices that preserve them, on which we should center our attention.

Since Putnam's stewardship, the Library has been directed by four Librarians of Congress. The poet Archibald MacLeish was appointed by his friend, Franklin D. Roosevelt, and MacLeish streamlined the Library's administration and programs. He is credited with pulling it abruptly into the twentieth century. President Harry S Truman appointed political scientist Luther H. Evans, who strengthened the Library's international links. President Dwight D. Eisenhower ap-

The Library's second building, the John Adams, opened in 1939.

A section
from the
Canterbury
Pilgrim
murals by
Ezra Winter
in the
Jefferson
Reading
Room

pointed Librarian L. Quincy Mumford, who greatly expanded the collections and the staff of the Library and increased its ties to the American library profession; and President Gerald Ford appointed historian Daniel J. Boorstin, who has expanded the Library's links with the literary and creative groups in the nation and emphasized the national role of the institution.

THE THIRD BUILDING
OF THE LIBRARY OF CONGRESS

With the great increase in materials and staff during the fifties and sixties, it became clear that the then two buildings could never support the activities assigned to the Library by the Congress. Library collections were housed in outlying airplane hangars and trucking warehouses, and the staff of complete programs were scattered in over a dozen locations in the District, Virginia and Maryland. Designing for a third building began in the early sixties with the expectation that it would be located on the block to the east of "the Annex"—"behind the two libraries." However, before the work was very far along, members of the House suggested that the Library be

THE GROUND OF LIBERTY IS TO BE GAINED BY INCHES · WE MUST BE CONTENTED TO SECURE WHAT WE CAN GET FROM TIME TO TIME AND ETERNALLY PRESS FORWARD FOR WHAT IS YET TO GET · IT TAKES TIME TO PERSUADE MEN TO DO EVEN WHAT IS FOR THEIR OWN GOOD .

A portion of the murals by Ezra Winter, dedicated to Thomas Jefferson, in the Jefferson Reading Room

combined with a memorial to the fourth president of the United States, James Madison, who had no monument in Washington in spite of the great role he had played in the creation of the Constitution and the concept of a federated republic. The result of this movement was the James Madison Memorial Building which now lies to the south of the original Library, the Thomas Jefferson Building.

The Madison building is the largest library building in the world—indeed only the Pentagon and the F.B.I. buildings are larger among all the U.S. government properties. It is designed for modern information storage and transfer. It has great computer installations with every floor and room wired for television and computer data transmission. Designed in modern modular style, walls are moveable, and space is infinitely flexible.

As a library, it has the unusual aspect of having no "stack area" as such. All floors are sufficiently strong to support books in any quantity at any point. With the third building, a division of labor has developed among the three installations: the Jefferson building has the public spaces—displays, exhibits, the general reading rooms, and the auditoriums and pavilions for public affairs; the Adams building is essentially the storage building, holding two-thirds of all the Library's books; and the Madison building houses those parts of the staff which operate essentially self-contained programs (the Congressional Research Service, Processing, and Copyright). The Madison also has the James Madison memorial halls which contain the portrait statue and exhibits associated with his political life. Immediately contiguous to the memorial are the Law Library and the Manuscript Division reflecting and reinforcing Madison's role in the nation's history.

Except for the Madison memorial area and a contiguous atrium, the Madison building is unornamented and crisply functional—the very antithesis of the original Library of Congress Building. Cafeteria areas on the top floor (where visitors to the Library are welcome) are decorated by walls of glass which open out on striking

Art deco
ornamentation
and design
in the John
Adams
Building

34

vistas of Washington City. The effect is a far cry from Mr. Blashfield's rotunda collar of togaed goddesses and "Human Understanding floating over Finite Intellectual Achievements." Times change, and the Library is approaching its third century.

BEHIND THE SCENES AT THE LIBRARY OF CONGRESS

The Library of Congress is much like a university in which certain "schools" serve certain disciplines or clienteles, and become small

The entrance to the third Library building, the James Madison Memorial, is ornamented with a bronze cascade of falling books by sculptor Frank Eliscu.

One of the quotations from President Madison in the James Madison Memorial Building

The James Madison statue by Walter K. Hancock; Madison is depicted at the age of 36 during the Constitutional Convention.

Fountain sculpture by Robert Cronbach in the Atrium of the James Madison Memorial Building

worlds in themselves. The Library serves six such worlds through six organizational units. The Congressional Research Service serves the Congress—exclusively. It works only for Congress and will not even respond to queries from the executive branch or the judiciary. Processing Services serves both the library world and the Library of Congress itself in its task of acquiring and organizing the knowledge of the world so it can be found when needed. The National Library Service for the Blind and Physically Handicapped brings the world of literature and factual information to those for whom a book or a television tape are inappropriate. The Copyright Office serves the creative elites of the country, guarding their inspiration and shielding their sometimes evanescent product from theft and exploitation. The Law Library serves the legal world. And finally, Research Services serves the scholars and scientific world by caring for the collections of the Library and assisting the users as they seek the preserved knowledge and experience that is the Library of Congress.

For the scientist or scholar who comes to the Library, the nineteen reading rooms of the institution become the open stage where they will do their work, and each of these is described, with suggestions about how to use each one most efficiently, in the second half of this guide. The other areas become, because they are not "public" in the usual sense of a public or college library dealing with a full spectrum of patrons, in effect "behind the scenes." What does the Library do in those parts which are not generally available to the visitor? A short description of some of these more specialized areas follows.

The Congressional Research Service

The Congressional Research Service (CRS) works exclusively for the Congress, and in many ways is the present day form of what the entire Library of Congress was when it began. It deals in an enormous quantity of information transfers in the course of a congressional year. These transfers can be as short as a how much, or how many, or when, or who question on one hand, to an exhaustive analysis of some public issue involving a dozen specialists, complicated computer modeling, and extensive publications on the other. Any of these forms becomes an "inquiry" and in an average year, the CRS will receive and answer over four hundred and fifty thousand such inquiries—over seventeen hundred every working day.

There are certain characteristics of the work that the CRS does for the Congress that make it different from usual research in a public library.

1. When the CRS is asked a question, either short or extended, it searches until it finds the answer and then transmits it—it does not simply get the materials and send them over saying, the reply is in these books. The CRS finds the reply, calculates the projection, makes the comparison and either talks to the inquiring member personally or prepares a specific response in writing.

2. The work is done under tight time pressure. Many of the queries come up in the course of floor debate and the answer must be found before the vote is called or the members leave the floor. Similarly, the congressional legislative attention moves from one topic to the next in sequential order. Thus, a certain number of days are allocated to the annual foreign aid bill, the next Medicaid amendments, and the immediate appropriation act. During these days hearings will be held, debate pursued, and the vote taken. Once the vote is concluded, that topic is ignored for another year, sometimes for a complete Congress. The CRS must be able to cope with all the questions that pour in on that topic during that small window of time, because any answer transmitted after the hearing or the vote is worthless.

3. The result of the time pressure requires that the CRS anticipate what will probably be needed weeks and often months before it is called for. Reports and studies are developed and loaded into the computer's memory, and they are then updated again and again so that they are ready to be printed out on command when required.

4. Finally, the CRS's work for the Congress must be unbiased, detached, and without recommendation. The CRS provides options, accumulates various cases pro and con, and tries to secure all the possible information and data that would be useful in reaching a policy decision—but the decision must be made by the member of Congress alone. The CRS does not advocate or endorse.

These four characteristics produce a department with unusual staffing and delivery skills. The CRS employs approximately 850 people, less than a tenth of whom are librarians. The remainder are specialists in certain fields needed to understand public issues: among them are petroleum geologists, biologists, welfare specialists, lawyers, and transportation specialists. The seven divisions into which they are grouped suggest the general subject areas that are covered for the Congress: American Law, Economics, Education and Public Welfare, Environment and Natural Resources Policy, Foreign Affairs and National Defense, Government, and Science Policy Research.

Since speed and currency are so important, the various devices for updating and transmitting the information are unusual. The CRS lays claim to a substantial portion of the Library's main computer into which it daily loads information on legislation and specific public issues, a magazine indexing program, and access to the Library's computerized main catalog. These programs can be retrieved on over 1,500 electronic terminals in the Library itself, and on an additional thousand-plus cathode ray tubes in the offices of the Senate and the House of Representatives. Special CRS reference centers are located in each of the five congressional office buildings, and hourly deliveries shuttle queries and replies back and forth between the Library and the legislature.

The CRS thus concentrates on fast information transfer and long-range policy analysis. There is a third area of its responsibility that has grown extensively in recent years—training new congressional staff in the legislative process.

The personal staffs of the legislators tend to "turn over" constantly—new faces arriving from home districts, eager to learn how Congress works as quickly as possible so they can reach maximum effectiveness in the shortest possible time. These newly arrived staff members come from three major sources: in some instances a member may have brought a particular specialist into his staff to assist him in writing a new piece of legislation of interest to his home community, and then to help him in getting the bill through the legislative process to passage; the new staff member can be a part of the nearly two thousand interns working in the offices from a month to a year or

The La Follette Congressional Reading Room in the James Madison Memorial Building

so each; and then the normal turnover from elections every two years brings a stream of new people to Capitol Hill. The result of all these elements is the arrival of a very large number of new staff each year, adding up to a substantial proportion of the 22,000 Congressional employees.

To help these newcomers learn the legislative process, the CRS sponsors weekly seminars and puts hourly lectures on videotape and plays them daily on the closed circuit congressional television. It stages mock congressional sessions at two- and three-day training institutes throughout the year. The CRS also publishes pro and con summaries of current legislative topics, distributes audio-tape cassette lectures that can be listened to in the staff members' cars coming to and from work, or via earphones on airplanes as they shuttle back and forth to their districts.

And in all these devices and the techniques it uses to keep the members current about national problems and aware of the maximum number of ways available for solving them, the CRS is acting as a direct descendant of those early librarians "just down the hall" in 1801.

Processing Services

Essentially all libraries have an organizational unit called "Technical Processes" or "Acquisitions and Cataloging" that secures the materials the library keeps and then organizes them for use. Not only is the Library of Congress no exception, its Processing Services department is the largest in the world with a staff of more than fifteen hundred people.

As in any library, no matter what size, the first step is to acquire the materials. In the case of the Library of Congress, this is relatively easy thanks to procedures established by the present staff's predecessors over the past 150 years. Most of the materials come in "automatically"—that is, channels have been established, and the products flow in with the Library playing an essentially passive role. The primary source of materials (in terms of use) comes from the copyright deposit—500,000 items a year, from which the Library takes about 400,000 to add to its collections. These materials are not only copies of all new bookstore books, but computer programs, all forms of music, ballet choreography, colored etchings, syndicated television shows, current motion pictures, telephone directories, and loose-leaf legal services.

The second source of the Library's materials is from government exchange and "official donation." The Library endeavors to collect and keep all the official documents of foreign governments, state

governments, and such quasi-governmental entities as the New York Port Authority, the Tennessee Valley Authority, international whaling commissions, and Antarctic arbitration committees. To get these exchange materials, the Library offers U.S. government documents to the trading partner, and the opposite government sends its materials, free, in return. The U.S. Government Printing Office gives the Library four complete sets of U.S. documents for itself, and all these governmental sources bring in 4.5 million items a year.

Next, *gifts* from private individuals, such as rare incunabula and other treasures from collectors like Lessing J. Rosenwald or huge sets of personal files like those from Henry Kissinger or Margaret Mead, will bring in two to three million pieces in any one year. A remaining two million items will come from transfers from other federal agencies and from the *purchase* of world newspapers. Newspapers, of which the Library keeps 1,700 current and daily, are rarely copyrighted and do not come by any of the other free, automatic devices.

While these channels may be "automatic" over the long pull, they must constantly be tended and new ones opened as new nations appear in the General Assembly, new federal agencies are born or combined, or new museums and institutes open in distant parts of the world. This endless work is carried on by the Acquisitions and Overseas Operations units.

Once the materials are within the Library, the next team of specialists begins to examine each of the ten million items to see if it appears to contain significant information and have lasting value. Space is expensive, binding is expensive, cataloging and computer input are expensive; materials cannot just be casually added to the collections for perpetual preservation. The selections officers must also check for such mundane concerns as, Is this a duplicate? Have other copies arrived from a different source? Is it a reprint?, an unimportant translation of something already in the Library?, a changed format from hardbound book to paperback to film strip to microfilm to taped cassette to videodisc?

Once the item has been selected for permanent addition to the collections, it passes on to the cataloging specialists. The book is first "described"—the author differentiated (usually by birth dates) from others of the same name, the title recorded, the printing history captured in the imprint, and now in the days of computer search there are internal identifications. Does it have maps, an index, a bibliography, illustrations? With the powerful logic of the Library's computer, it is possible to say, "I want to see books about the San Andreas fault, but only those in English, published since 1970, which contain maps and a bibliography." The descriptive cataloging divisions provide these identifying marks.

The book then passes to the subject catalogers who determine what it is about. Consistent subject headings are determined and affixed. (Shall it be put under canaries, cage birds, songbirds, finches, aviaries, or pets?) The Library's printed cards are sold by the millions for smaller libraries' catalogs, and for these the subject headings must be limited to the most precise to prevent flooding smaller catalogs with "added entries"; on the other hand, with more and more libraries holding their records in digital storage, the more "tags" that can be placed on an entry, the more ways its contents can be revealed and made useful. The great card catalog seen in the Main Reading Room indexes the books secured from 1800 to 1981. At that point it was "closed"—no more cards inserted—and the Library's computer became the sole approach to the general book collections. Cathode ray tube terminals can be seen in use throughout the public reading rooms of the Library.

In addition to the subject headings, the subject catalogers must also affix a "call number" to each volume, so the books can be placed on shelves and sit among other books about the same subject. This is called "classification" and most local libraries use the Dewey Decimal System to organize their collections. The Library of Congress was one of the last libraries in the nation to assign any classed numbers to its holdings, and to Librarian Young's distress in 1898, he found that the Library had grown so large already that the Dewey system would be meaningless (whole floors of books would have had the same number, among other problems). The catalogers of the time set out to devise a new scheme "just for the Library." Using far more restricted and precise breakdowns, the Library developed the Library of Congress Classification scheme in 35 volumes, and since that time more and more of the nation's largest collections have shifted over to the LC scheme. Nowadays, the Library selects a single number (actually two letters and up to twelve digits) for its Library of Congress call number, but the Library also assigns the appropriate Dewey Decimal number for collections that use this classification system. Only the former, of course, goes on the Library's copy of the book.

Subject cataloging skills are complex. (Should a book about Joan of Arc be placed with books about French history, famous women, the Hundred Years War, martyrs, saints, the English in Calais, Henry VI, medieval strategy and tactics, or the Catholic Church? What if it is a movie script about Joan, a play in verse, or pictures of her portraits as expressed in oils? Same number? Which one?)

Tied up with all aspects of acquisitions and cataloging is the language problem. The Library receives books in 470 different languages and less than a fourth of a year's receipts will be in English. The remainder must be both read and analyzed by someone who knows the language, and the catalog card must duplicate the script of the book. Japanese and Chinese cards are sent in script to Japan where they are converted to masters. The masters are returned to the Library and copied onto optical disks by laser scanning, and when

All Library of Congress cataloging data are now stored in the computer and copies are made available to outside libraries weekly by computer tape services.

copies of the cards are requested by American libraries, another laser drives a xerographic printer to make the requested sets. Other scripts are either actually printed in the original script—such as, Hebrew, Arabic, or Russian—or, if the characters are too esoteric to be re-printed, the language is transliterated and the words romanized. Eventually, all non-Roman scripts will be stored on optical disks.

The Processing Services librarians are not only acquiring and cata-loging the books and documents for the Library's own use, but they are also sharing their cataloging data with the entire library commu-nity. As a result, a catalog card from the smallest bookmobile to the largest university library is entered in precisely the same way so scho-lars—indeed the most casual reader—can find the item in a consistent and expected manner. In earlier times, this was done by selling the cards themselves to the smaller libraries. Now it comes about by the Library of Congress loading computer tapes with the same data it puts into its own system; these tapes (known as MARC for MAchine Readable Cataloging) are then purchased by regional library net-works and facilities in the United States and Canada. The networks in turn make the data available to their local libraries. The Library of Congress works with professional library associations throughout the country and abroad to establish useful and agreed-on cataloging rules, and it publishes new and updated lists of subject headings, Dewey Decimal numbers, and union catalogs to help with uniform standards throughout the professional library community.

Librarian of Congress Putnam back at the turn of the century, was convinced that (since the same book could turn up at ten thousand li-braries) once a book was deposited for copyright and cataloged by the Library of Congress, all libraries should use that cataloging and save themselves the time and expense of doing it again. This implied that the Library's cataloging would be of the highest quality, and that the Library would indeed get the material at the earliest point. Both of these standards have been met for over eighty years now, and Putnam's hopes have been realized. The only differences now are that 1) the printed card is being replaced by the computer disk and 2) the book is no longer the only way to capture knowledge. Microfiche are becoming a part of scholarly publishing. Optical disks provide new ways of cataloging art objects or training technicians or publishing encyclopedias. When linked to optical disks, a computer permits a kind of interaction with the material that is entirely different from anything we have known before. The Library is shifting to keep up with the new formats, but still trying to meet Putnam's demands to do it once and do it right (and let the local librarians concentrate on serving their immediate clienteles doing things that the Library can never hope to duplicate).

Programs for the Nation

It is too easy to think of the Library of Congress as a passive warehouse of books, waiting for someone to come to use them. While over a million readers do indeed come to use the collections each year, many of the programs take the books or their contents out of Washington to users around the nation.

The National Library Service for the Blind and Physically Handicapped   The most spectacular of these activities is the Library's program for blind and physically handicapped readers. Starting with 200 "raised letter" books in Librarian Young's special room for the blind (1897), it has grown to a $37 million program which in any one year will place books in the hands of a readership of more than six hundred thousand people. Every year some twenty-three hundred titles will be added to the collection on disc, cassette, or in braille.

Braille readers generally have been blind for most of their lives, in contrast to those who have lost their sight through illness, accidents, or complications of aging, and therefore most braille readers learned to read the symbols at an early age. For this reason, braille readers tend to be younger than the rest of the patrons, and frequently prefer the more innovative, experimental fiction and the more controversial of the nonfiction. Overall, of the tens of thousands of titles requested

The Library's National Library Service for the Blind and Physically Handicapped distributes books in braille throughout the nation.

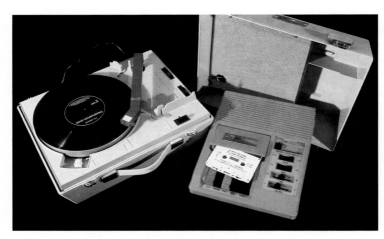

A talking book machine (left) and a cassette machine, which carry three and six hours of spoken text, respectively, on a single disc or tape.

and sent out to the total readership served by the program, about half will be best-sellers, popular fiction, biographies and how-to-do-it books, and the other half literary classics and standard works. The books are read onto the various devices by professional actors or narrators, and occasionally by the authors themselves, as in the case of Pearl Bailey, Art Buchwald, William F. Buckley, and Desi Arnaz.

The Library distributes seventy magazines, some in braille *(Better Homes and Gardens, Fortune, Popular Mechanics),* and others on light, flexible discs *(Atlantic, Sports Illustrated, U.S. News),* which are circulated to subscribers at approximately the same time print issues appear on newsstands. Like the books, all magazines are sent free on request. This suggests two questions: what are the machines the Library lends, and how does a visually or physically handicapped person gain access to the service?

The machines The program began with "talking books" which were records played on machines at the unusually slow speed (in 1934) of 33⅓ revolutions per minute. Since 1973, talking book records have been made to turn at only 8⅓ rpm, and they will carry three hours of narration on a ten-inch disc (when you look at them, they scarcely seem to move). These phonographs have been lent out, free, since 1943, delivered directly to the user by the post office.

The audio cassettes the program uses are equally in advance of their time, and the present tapes run at $^{15}/_{16}$ rpm on four tracks so a single cassette will carry nearly six hours of playing time, the equivalent of 200 pages of print. These cassettes will gradually replace the recorded discs, since cassettes play longer and can be produced more quickly and cheaply.

The Library offers a variety of playback equipment on free loan to satisfy the needs of a diverse group of users. In addition, the machines can be modified with a number of accessories to make them more convenient for the user: they come with headphones, pillow speakers for bedridden patrons, amplifiers for users with hearing disabilities, and special arms and attachments for those who have difficulty pushing buttons or inserting discs or cassettes.

The network Regional and local public libraries are the key to the entire distribution system. The Library of Congress selects the titles to be transcribed and sees that the tapes, records, and braille are made and duplicated. The various formats are then sent to central units (usually the state library or the largest public library) in each state. These serve either as regional libraries for their states, or they in turn designate local public libraries as distribution centers. Materials are shuttled back and forth through the system to get maximum advantage out of the thousands of titles ready to be used. The requester knows only that he asks for material from a single address and the material arrives in the mail at his own home (with the appropriate playback machine accompanying his first request).

The system works very efficiently. Monthly magazines are received as soon as the print versions appear on the newsstands, bestsellers are available almost as quickly as they are reviewed, and if a book is not immediately available, every effort is made to produce it. There are thousands of volunteers assisting in every state. Local braillists and narrators, many of them trained or certified by the Library, work in their own communities producing books and special materials on request (often for students). And senior and retired telephone industry employees (The Telephone Pioneers of America) repair thousands of playback machines every year without charge. In fact, the entire program is operated free of charge for the user.

How does a visually or physically handicapped person become a part of the lending service? He or she need only call the local public library and express interest. The librarian there either will have tapes or records in stock or will tell the inquirer where the nearest regional distribution center is located. It is not complicated to become a part of the program. Anyone who has any kind of visual or physical impairment that prevents the reading of normal print is eligible, and an application form signed by a doctor or social worker will suffice. Again, the local library should have the forms to apply, but if not, you may write the National Library Service for the Blind and Physically

48

A variety of devices by which written materials are made available to the blind and physically handicapped

Handicapped, Library of Congress, Washington, D.C. 20542, for the required application.

The Children's Literature Center   The Library owns over 300,000 children's books from the earliest forms of printing to the latest videodisks—and the materials come from every country of the world. It has a special reading room and staff to enhance the usefulness of the children's media, but the specialists here concentrate on adults, not on the children directly.

The Center works with children's book authors and illustrators; with publishers, librarians, and scholars. The children benefit indirectly from the help the Library gives to teachers, editors, parents, and others who work with youth.

The Center creates its own publications. It selects an annual booklist, as well as catalogs and guides to children's materials, and it sponsors lectures and special programs designed to focus attention on the current thinking and publishing in the children's media fields. Its links are broad, working as closely with television and motion picture creators as with the more traditional book and library practitioners.

The Juilliard Quartet Concerts   We have been noting some of the
ways the Library of Congress goes "out of its walls" and takes its services and holdings *to* the nation, and nothing it does accomplishes
this as gracefully as the music broadcasts from the Coolidge Auditorium. Thanks to the distribution of tapes to classical music stations in
the past and present-day broadcasting via satellite, to many people
"The Library of Congress" means fine sound as well as fine books.
The story of how this came about goes back to a remarkable series of
events stimulated by a series of remarkable people. It started with the
gift of an auditorium.

The first person involved was a woman, Elizabeth Sprague Coolidge, who had been a pianist and composer herself, and then had
become a leading patron of chamber music in the years after World
War I. She created the Berkshire Concerts held annually on South
Mountain in Massachusetts and, once these had become popular and
successful, later turned to the nation's capital as a more central site to
give prominence to the genre. In 1925, working with Librarian
Putnam and with the blessings of Congress, she gave the money and
the plans for a complete auditorium to be built in the empty Library
courtyard outside the Librarians's office. When the hall was completed, it seated 511 people, was designed especially for chamber
music, had an elevator which would bring a full-size concert grand
from the Library basement up onto the stage, and—most wondrous of
all—it proved to have almost perfect acoustics for the projection and
enjoyment of chamber music. It is one of the finest halls of its kind in
the world.

Mrs. Coolidge supplemented the gift of the auditorium with the establishment of a fund of money (the Library's first endowment)
which was called the Coolidge Foundation and was designed to un-
derwrite chamber music performances. Free "sellouts" became a tradition in the Washington cultural scene, and Coolidge money has created a continuing series of new chamber works through fifty years of
commissions to contemporary composers.

In the 1930s, the second patron appeared, Gertrude Clarke Whittall. Although she and Mrs. Coolidge had never met, Mrs. Whittall
was in such agreement with Mrs. Coolidge's purposes that she
ordered a music dealer to find and buy five Stradivari instruments
which she gave to the Library along with an additional endowment to
buy rare manuscripts of chamber works. The money has since brought
the Library such treasures as two Bach cantatas, the sketches for portions of two Beethoven quartets (the second movement of opus 130
and the last movement of opus 131), and a remarkable collection of

Schoenberg compositions. In addition to these purchases, Mrs. Whittall also gave money for a room—the Whittall Pavilion—which houses the instruments when they are not in use for concerts and rehearsals.

The care of rare and antique musical instruments has long been a concern in the musical world. Mrs. Whittall was determined that her five Strads would be used, and a part of her agreement of deposit was that the instruments would be played regularly, throughout each year, to keep them from becoming mere museum pieces.

Immediately on receipt of the instruments, the Library set out to satisfy Mrs. Whittall's wishes but it found, to its surprise, that while musicians were eager to play in the Coolidge Auditorium, they were much less enthusiastic about playing with unfamiliar instruments. There being so little time to become used to the tone, handling, and musical characteristics of the rarities, performers preferred to use their own instruments. Historical events provided the solution.

The five Stradivari had been given in 1935, and soon thereafter the internationally famous Budapest Quartet fled Nazi Germany. The Chief of the Library's Music Division, Harold Spivacke, conceived the idea of using the group as a quartet-in-residence, who would become familiar with the instruments and could perform concerts throughout a nine-month season. The Budapest accepted the offer and began a distinguished relationship with the Library in the late thirties which lasted until 1962 when their role was assumed by the Juilliard String Quartet, which is carrying on the tradition with honor and acclaim to this day.

The celebrated Juilliard String Quartet playing the Library's Stradivari instruments in the Coolidge Auditorium

Five Stradivari instruments were given to the Library by Gertrude Clarke Whittall —shown are two of the three violins, a viola, and a cello.

The next step came in 1950 when Dr. Serge Koussevitzky, the long-time conductor of the Boston Symphony Orchestra, created the Serge Koussevitzky Music Foundation in the Library of Congress. In 1942, Koussevitzky had begun to commission new works—including Bartók's Concerto for Orchestra and Britten's opera, *Peter Grimes*—in memory of his wife, Natalie. Once established in the Library, the Foundation proceeded to commission such major compositions as the Seventh Symphony of Roy Harris, Francis Poulenc's *Gloria*, and Douglas Moore's opera, *The Ballad of Baby Doe*.

In 1970, the Koussevitzky funds were followed by an additional gift of money from Leonora Jackson McKim. She was an internationally famous concert violinist who established the McKim Fund in the Library for commissioning and presenting chamber music for violin and piano.

All of the above gifts added together have permitted the Library to present a wide variety of performers and instruments. The dozens of programs throughout the year thus offer music running the full spectrum from traditional repertoire to new compositions. The Library wants this music to have the widest possible audience, and with the help of Washington patrons of music, the concerts are recorded and made available to "good music stations" across the country.

The Poetry Consultant   The Coolidge Auditorium hears words as well as music, since the world-famed poetry readings of the Library are also staged there. The Library acquired its poetic role through one of Librarian Putnam's "Chairs" which he filled with "consultants to the Library" to help him strengthen and exploit the collections. The Consultant in Poetry in English became one of the best known of these, and through the years has brought to the Library a truly breathtaking list of some of the leading figures in American literature. The following have filled their terms with vigorous programs, broadening the public's knowledge of their craft.

Joseph Auslander	1937-41	Howard Nemerov	1963-64
Allen Tate	1943-44	Reed Whittemore	1964-65
Robert Penn Warren	1944-45	Stephen Spender	1965-66
Louise Bogan	1945-46	James Dickey	1966-68
Karl Shapiro	1946-47	William Jay Smith	1968-70
Robert Lowell	1947-48	William E. Stafford	1970-71
Leonie Adams	1948-49	Josephine Jacobsen	1971-73
Elizabeth Bishop	1949-50	Daniel Hoffman	1973-74
Conrad Aiken	1950-52	Stanley Kunitz	1974-76
Randall Jarrell	1956-58	Robert Hayden	1976-78
Robert Frost	1958-59	William Meredith	1978-80
Richard Eberhart	1959-61	Maxine Kumin	1981-82
Louis Untermeyer	1961-63	Anthony Hecht	1982-84
		Robert Fitzgerald	1984-85

The Poetry Lounge, furnished with antiques given by Gertrude Clarke Whittall, is used as a reception room by the Poetry Consultant.

Exhibitions, Publications, and Tapes Another aspect of the Library's programs for the nation is making known what is in the Library of Congress. This involves two different kinds of preserved objects: the great treasures and shared works of art whether they be patriotic, historical, or aesthetic on the one hand; and the raw, colorless data on the other. These data lie there as records, diaries, scientific readings, and unpublished charts that, if the proper professional elites could know of their existence, might be a missing link, the absent piece of the puzzle.

The Library tries to meet this challenge in a variety of ways.

The great Jefferson building was designed as a museum, and with the opening of the Madison building the Library was able to move out desks and files and people and once again reclaim exhibit space which had been lost for two generations. This has permitted the renewed display of some of the rarest items in the collections. The new Madison halls themselves permit rotating, special exhibits in multiple locations, while the older buildings support revelations of specific formats. Thus, at any given time, a visitor may come upon a display about cowboy life (from the American Folklife Center), or see rare turn-of-the-century color photographs made decades before our modern dye prints (materials from the Prints and Photographs Division). There has been a multiroomed presentation of the history of paper; another of the illustrated book. The spaces permit variety. Current photography from the annual White House News Photographers' competition can be contrasted with genre engravings of the nine-

A panel from the Library's Fifty Years of Animation exhibition, highlighting Disney materials from the Library's collections

54

Khmer Classical Dancers performing at an American Folklife Center outdoor concert, September 3, 1981

teenth century or political cartoons of the eighteenth. Rare prints of Durer or Rembrandt are mounted beside the latest abstract and colorist prints received in last month's acquisitions. Similarly, historical events—the Emancipation Proclamation, the moon landings, a half century of Walt Disney art—can be presented, elaborated on, and linked to the multiple, associated holdings spread throughout the collections.

Once these exhibits have been shared with the Washington community, the Library makes them available to other libraries and museums around the country. Thus the original items from the Library's holdings are seen in home communities where the magical sense of presence is added to the statement that these artifacts exist and are part of our heritage.

An equally effective way of sharing the one-of-a-kind treasures is the preparation and publishing of high quality facsimiles of the pieces. These are in fact "duplicates"—the same size as the original, reproduced with great care and multiple color plates, on paper toned to match the original piece. When the technique is applied to large maps such as Samuel de Champlain's *Map of the Northeast Coast of North America*, 1607; Battista Agnese's *Map of the World*, ca. 1544; Johannes Vingboons's *Map of Manhattan*, 1639; or the *Chart of the Mediterranean Sea and Western Europe*, 1559, drawn by Mateus Prunes, the facsimiles become valuable tools for study as well as fine wall prints for the decoration of homes and libraries. At distances beyond a few feet, they cannot be told from the original.

The Library has done the same thing with musical manuscripts like the Brahms *Concerto for Violin*, Mozart's *Gran Partita*, and Mendelssohn's *Octet for Strings*: and such historical volumes as *The 1812 Catalogue of the Library of Congress* and *The Journal of Gideon Olmsted, Adventures of a Sea Captain during the American Revolution.*

In addition to these rarities, the Library tries to select items which are aesthetically important in themselves—regardless of their historical associations. These are made into posters, greeting cards, calendars, and wrapping paper, so the images can be made familiar around the country.

The raw data, on the other hand, must be revealed through books. The Library publishes such volumes as *Special Collections in the Library of Congress, Bookbinding and the Conservation of Books, Historic America, Railroad Maps of North America, Letters of Delegates to Congress, 1774-1789*, and *James Madison and the Search for Nationhood.* A catalog of over six hundred Library of Congress publications in print can be received free by writing the Library.

It should be recalled that nearly a quarter of a million books are lent

Some of the books, facsimiles, reproductions, greeting cards, and postcards published by the Library

from the Library of Congress to local libraries each year under "interlibrary loan" programs, and high fidelity tapes of the fifty free Juilliard concerts are played the year round on fine arts stations. Cable television producers are using Library of Congress materials in ever-mounting numbers which, in turn, is letting the nation see what is in the collections and suggesting applications to local research that would not have been possible a decade ago.

The Copyright Office

The Library of Congress has been in the copyright business for over a hundred years. It did not invent the idea, however, as is frequently assumed. The first copyright law was passed by the British Parliament in 1709, and tradition has it that the statute was based on a draft written by Jonathan Swift. The copyright law protects artists, authors, and thinkers against the theft of their creations. Nowadays one can get copyright protection for such kinds of things as books, music, plays, dance choreography, paintings, sculptures, motion pictures, and sound recordings. It also protects computer programs, architectural blueprints, and maps. (You *cannot* copyright titles of books or slogans or general processes or procedures. There also can be no copyright for standard calendars, blank forms, or U.S. government publications.)

The Library of Congress got into the copyright business primarily in order to get free material for the Library's collections, but through-

The official
Copyright
Seal of the
United States

out all the years since, the Librarians of Congress have taken great pride in the Library's role in making copyright in this country simple, prompt, and in the best interest of the creative artist. Spofford's original version of the copyright law was passed in 1870. This stayed in force without much change until 1909 when adjustments were made, and then another half century passed without significant modification. In 1955 the Congress asked the Copyright Office for help in bringing the law into line with modern practices, and ultimately a major revision was passed that took effect in 1978. By the time the new legislation was enacted, it was forced to take cognizance of cable television, satellite transmission, jukeboxes, and impersonal corporate creativity.

How do you register something for copyright? You must first secure the proper form from the Copyright Office, Library of Congress, Washington, D.C. 20559. Tell them what kind of work you want registered—such as, a poem, piece of music, or poster—so they can send you the correct form. There is no charge for the forms.

Once you have the proper form, it should be filled out and put in a single envelope or package with a check or money order for ten dollars and a copy for deposit of the work being registered. If the work has been published, generally you must deposit two copies. The envelope or package is then mailed to the address noted above, where it will be processed, and a formal registration returned to you.

Not only books are copyrighted, but computer programs, architectural blueprints, dance choreography, and, as in these deposits, board games.

Does the Library keep everything it gets by copyright? No. When they come in, the registered pieces are offered to the Library and its selection officers pick out those items which meet the Library's acquisition standards. In an average year, over half a million works are copyrighted; from these the Library will usually take about four hundred thousand for its general collections. In terms of later use, these copyrighted materials will prove to be the ones most frequently requested and drawn from the shelves, although they represent less than 5 percent of the Library's annual acquisitions.

The copyright receipt has had an interesting, democratizing effect on the Library's collections. Traditionally, since a library has only a certain amount of money to spend, it sets out to acquire the best, the "cream" of a year's books, music, and drama. Being human, the selectors and acquirers define this "cream" by their own standards and tastes; this has been true since the French and Austrian kings began to assemble public libraries in the 1600s. Traditionally, therefore, most libraries are made up of what the current generation thought was the best, the most valuable, and would be the longest lasting.

However, because the copyright deposit brought in "everything" (and, in fact, the Library has kept almost everything that was keepable), it has covered the creative products of America detached from the personal taste of the successive librarians. For this reason, the Library has more plain, ordinary photography from the Civil War period and from the opening of the West than any other collection in the world. The great collections kept the best of the Western exploratory photography. The Library of Congress kept everything that was sent in by the commercial exploring parties for copyright protection. Similarly, the music copyright deposits reflect what the ordinary composers were writing, not just those who were commercially successful or lucky enough to be recognized. In the nineteenth and early twentieth centuries, most music librarians kept classical and drawing room music; the Library of Congress kept everything it got, meaning that in many cases it has the only copies now extant of nineteenth-century dance music, ballads, minstrel songs, and ragtime.

Records of the registration of all this material can be found in the Copyright Card Catalog, which is open to the public. The works are cataloged under author, title, and claimant (not by subject), and arrangements can be made to inspect the materials themselves in the Copyright Office, if they have not been taken for the general Library collections.

The Copyright Office employs over five hundred persons and handles enormous quantities of materials and inquiries promptly and with a minimum of red tape. The various data which have been accumulating for over a hundred years now are being transferred to the computer, and the whole process from jukebox registration to videodisc deposits is going on-line, digitally stored.

THE LIBRARY'S TREASURES

In the course of accumulating the world's knowledge, it was inevitable that the Library would acquire many rare and precious items of man's intellectual efforts. In fact, through the generosity of individual donors, the Library has become a museum celebrating the creative genius. There are over two thousand unique and startling examples of this in the Library's collections, and these special treasures are circulated through the display cases and exhibit areas so at any one time a visitor will see some examples, although, of course, not all. Some of the kinds of things that a visitor may expect to see are suggested below. While one might expect rare incunabula and medieval portolans, the Library takes equal pride in such less likely pieces as the earliest motion picture print (Fred Ott's *Sneeze*, made by Thomas Edison in 1893) and the original manuscripts of such musical theater as *Porgy and Bess, Show Boat, West Side Story,* and *Oklahoma!*, and all the Victor Herbert operettas, all in their composers' own handwriting.

For Americans, probably the Library's greatest treasure is Thomas Jefferson's Rough Draft of the Declaration of Independence. The Draft consists of four pen and ink pages which were Jefferson's original working copy, written in June of 1776, of America's first state paper. Before bringing the finished text before the Continental Congress, Jefferson showed it to Benjamin Franklin and John Adams, who made changes in their own handwriting directly on the draft pages. The draft then went to the Congress where some eighty changes were made as the result of floor debate; and these, too, appear on these remarkable sheets as deletions, interpolations, and marginal corrections. Jefferson, incidentally, wrote "inalienable rights" and it left the chamber in this form; someone on the way to the printer changed this to the "unalienable," which appears in the traditional text.

The Library owns the personal papers of most of the presidents from Washington to Coolidge and has, in addition, great quantities of associated memorabilia from such figures as Lincoln, Theodore Roosevelt, and Woodrow Wilson. In the case of Abraham Lincoln, for example, the library owns the handwritten draft of the Emancipation Proclamation and has *two* handwritten copies of the Gettysburg Address—the one Lincoln held in his hand when he gave the speech

A Declaration by the Representatives of the UNITED STATES
OF AMERICA, in General Congress assembled.

When in the course of human events it becomes necessary for one people to
dissolve the political bands which have connected them with another, and to ~~assume among the powers of the earth that equal &~~ as
-sume among the powers of the earth the separate and equal ~~&~~ station to
which the laws of nature & of nature's god entitle them, a decent respect
to the opinions of mankind requires that they should declare the causes
which impel them to the separation.

We hold these truths to be self-evident; that all men ar
created equal & ~~independent~~ that ~~from that equal creation they derive~~ ~~rights~~ they are endowed by their creator with equal
~~inherent & inalienable, among these are~~ rights; that these
life, & liberty, & the pursuit of happiness; that to secure these rights, governments are instituted among men, deriving their just powers from
the consent of the governed; that whenever any form of government
~~shall~~ becomes destructive of these ends, it is the right of the people to alter
or to abolish it, & to institute new government, laying it's foundation on
such principles & organising it's powers in such form, as to them shall
seem most likely to effect their safety & happiness. prudence indeed
will dictate that governments long established should not be changed for
light & transient causes: and accordingly all experience hath shewn that
mankind are more disposed to suffer while evils are sufferable, than to
right themselves by abolishing the forms to which they are accustomed. but
when a long train of abuses & usurpations [begun at a distinguished period
&] pursuing invariably the same object, evinces a design to ~~subject~~ reduce
them under absolute Despotism, it is their right, it is their duty, to throw off such
+ & to provide new guards for their future security. such has
been the patient sufferance of these colonies; & such is now the necessity
which constrains them to expunge their former systems of government.
the history of the present king of Great Britain is a history of unremitting injuries and
usurpations, among which appears no solitary fact to contra-
-dict the uniform tenor of the rest all of which have in direct object the
establishment of an absolute tyranny over these states. to prove this, let facts be
submitted to a candid world, for the truth of which we pledge a faith
yet unsullied by falsehood.

One of the greatest treasures of the Library of Congress is the Rough Draft of the Declaration of Independence in Thomas Jefferson's own hand.

and a copy he wrote out for John Wills, his host in Pennsylvania for the occasion. Rather astonishingly, the Library owns the contents of Lincoln's pockets when he died. They were given to the Library by Lincoln's granddaughter and include two pairs of gold-rimmed spectacles, a pocket knife, and a loose watch fob made of gold-bearing quartz. His billfold contained a five-dollar Confederate note and nine newspaper clippings, all praising the president for various actions he had taken while in office.

The Library owns thousands of items relating to the Revolution and the founding of the republic, including the Washington-Cornwallis Articles of Capitulation at Yorktown, signed by both generals; and the rare "Notes of Debates in the Federal Convention," Madi-

The Giant Bible of Mainz is the last great hand-illuminated manuscript Bible, its margins decorated with incredibly detailed birds, animals, and flowers.

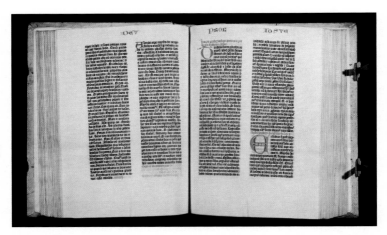

The first book printed with movable metal type, the Gutenberg Bible is also one of the world's finest examples of bookmaking.

son's handwritten record of the proceedings leading up to the creation of the Constitution.

Some unusual items appear in the handwriting of the great, often scribbled on cheap tablets or the backs of envelopes. Some examples of this are the Library's manuscript of Walt Whitman's *Leaves of Grass* (the only page still existing of the original draft; while the remainder were used to start his fireplace, this page survived because of a list of words he had scribbled on the back). The Library owns Alexander Graham Bell's original working sketch of the telephone, his "instrument for the transmission of vocal utterance by telegraph," as he called it at the time; as well as the first transcription of a telegraph message, the famous strip of paper lettering "What hath God wrought?" by Samuel F. B. Morse in 1844.

The pictorial treasures run the gamut of every place and most times. The Library owns the earliest picture of the Capitol taken in 1846. It also owns the earliest portrait of Abraham Lincoln taken the same year, when he was thirty-seven. It has all of the original photographs taken by the Wright Brothers recording their first successful powered flights at Kitty Hawk (as well as many unsuccessful tries ending in glider crashes). The pictures go backwards in time. The Library has a beautifully illustrated Chinese scroll printed in 975; it is 68 feet long and 6½ inches wide.

It has the carefully drawn, watercolored earliest known map of Manhattan Island, which was prepared for the West India Company of Holland in 1639. Staten Eylant is clearly marked, but the Hudson appears as Noort Rivier. It has an equally beautiful map of the northeast coast of North America drawn by Samuel de Champlain himself in 1607 after exploring the region. He marked on the map where he anchored each night, and noted the sites of the Indian villages he encountered. The Library's map collection is, in fact, the largest in the world, and contains such rarities as a portolan chart of the Mediterranean drawn between 1320 and 1350 which traces the shoreline between Spain and the Black Sea with astonishing accuracy, and two magnificent Coronelli globes that stand over five feet tall. The latter were created by the Cartographer to the Venetian Republic in 1692, and while being works of both beauty and precision, they are also the largest printed globes ever made before our own time.

Probably the most extensive group of rarities falls in the Lessing J. Rosenwald collection of the illustrated book from the fifteenth to the twentieth century. Made up of over 2,500 precious items, it includes the Giant Bible of Mainz from 1453, one of the two known copies of the 1495 *Epistolae et Evangelia,* and rare products of William Caxton's press. The collection also includes hundreds of early examples of Rosenwald's personal interests: books on botany, calligraphy, chess, and science—and his comprehensive collection of William Blake drawings and engravings.

The Library's music collection contains both rare instruments and rare manuscripts. It owns over sixteen hundred flutes from cultures around the world (including Frederick the Great's own instrument in its handmade, porcelain case). It has the magnificent collection of Stradivarius stringed instruments mentioned above, a Guarnerius violin, and a handsome Amati. All of these instruments are played regularly, either in the public concerts or as practice instruments when recognized artists are searching the unpublished scores of the composers they seek. The Library's collection of musical material—the original, working manuscripts of the composers—is awesome. It owns the complete Brahms Violin Concerto with the emendations of Joseph Joachim mixed in with Brahms's and the manuscript of Liszt's First Piano Concerto with Liszt's changes pasted in paper flaps on top of each other as he corrected and developed. It also owns the manuscript of Beethoven's Piano Sonata in E Major opus 109, Haydn's Ninety-fourth Symphony (the *Surprise*), and Schumann's First Symphony (known as *The Spring*).

The final treasures which space permits noting are also the most celebrated. Located on either side of the entrance to the Main Reading Room in the Jefferson building are the two cases holding the Giant Bible of Mainz and the Gutenberg Bible. The Giant Bible of

The Gutenberg Bible is on display in a special case in the Library's Great Hall.

The distance of the first successful powered flight at Kitty Hawk on December 17, 1903 was 120 feet; Orville Wright was at the controls.

Mainz is considered by many scholars to be the finest example of a hand-lettered, medieval manuscript in existence. It was created in Mainz, Germany, between April 1452 (when the first page was completed) and June 1453 (the last). Not only is the lettering flawless, but the decorations on every page—Biblical scenes, animals, flowers, and portraits of churchmen and rulers—are without peer. In the same town and at precisely the same time as this great work of illumination was being drawn, Johann Gutenberg was inventing the technique of printing by individual, movable pieces of type—the invention which was to end the creation of hand-lettered books forever. The Library's Gutenberg Bible is one of three, perfect vellum copies in existence. The other two are in the British Museum and the Bibliotheque Nationale. In 1978 a paper copy of the book sold for $2.4 million.

The Bible represents one of the most astonishing inventions of technological man. In achieving the first book, Gutenberg had to develop a system by which a whole series of inventions or modifications came together successfully. The ink of the time was soot in water and ran through the type beds; the paper of the time was fluffy, absorbent, and like blotting paper; the only press known was one with which to crush grapes to make wine; and the nearest things to a piece of type were wood block pictures of the saints. Gutenberg had to hand carve individual letters to get his masters and then devise techniques by which all successive castings would be uniform in height and design so they would not punch the paper or print unevenly. He had to invent oil-based ink and hardened paper; and he modified the wine press into an instrument that was not changed again until the 1800s. The result of all these efforts is the book displayed in the Great Hall, a product so perfect both technologically and artistically that it is difficult to think of how it might be improved—and this on the first attempt with an untried invention.

PRESERVATION—
THE RACE AGAINST DISINTEGRATION

Once any item is selected for the collections, the Library promises to preserve it, care for it, essentially forever. The curse is that from the moment the Library receives it, it is trying to deteriorate to dust. The paper is becoming brittle, turning brown, and disintegrating. The movie films are getting hard, the emulsion is separating from the backing, the color dyes are fading. The ink on the manuscripts is getting dim, the microfilm is getting spots, binding thread is rotting, covers are splitting off. The race, therefore, becomes one of retarding where you can and transferring to better material when you must.

Preservation starts right in the processing cycle. One-half of all the printed items the Library receives are unbound, so they must be sent out to contractors to be bound in order to protect them from use and to keep their parts together as they age. Newspapers, which become brittle in months, not years, are immediately microfilmed in the Library's photoduplication laboratories, and the papers themselves are discarded. Motion pictures are rushed straight into the Library's refrigerated vaults and kept for their lifetime only a few degrees above freezing. Manuscripts are put in fumigating vaults and gassed to kill any present or future mold or insects. Once removed and rehumidified, they are then placed in nonacidic, metal-edged boxes, and stored on their sides in the Manuscript Division. Phonograph records are stored vertically, deliberately packed together so they constitute a block of vinyl three feet long to prevent warping. Maps are encased in polyester envelopes, as are theatrical posters and billboard sheets. Daguerreotypes are put between squares of glass, and photographs are put in protective sleeves.

But acid is the enemy. For the first thousand years, paper was made of rags, and this paper has held up remarkably well. It is still flexible, reasonably white, and holding together. (Although, just in the last two decades traffic fumes and institutional heating have started to penetrate the pages and when added to the moisture supplied by air conditioning, the antebellum books are filling with sulphuric acid and developing problems.) After 1860, however, mass publishing exceeded the supply of rags, and the papermakers turned to wood for the

The Library's Preservation Laboratory uses sophisticated equipment to determine how to save and restore the deteriorating materials in its collections.

fiber they needed. Wood is made of cellulose held together with lignin. When wood pulp is exposed to light the lignin turns brown and the paper loses its strength. The papermakers add chemicals to get the lignin out and alum to improve the printing surface—thereby generating more acids which make the paper weak and brittle.

These processes are creating nightmares in all the great libraries of the world. Books barely fifty years old are splintering and cracking and their pages are dropping out in minute flakes. The Library of Congress has been racing against this destruction for thirty years now, and over seven million pages are microfilmed each year, one page at a time, trying to capture the text before it is lost.

The Library's chemists, who have been searching for a method of preventing the damage before it starts, have recently devised this valuable technique: acidic, wood pulp books are placed in huge, space age vacuum tanks where they are flooded with diethyl zinc gas, thus deacidifying them for at least another hundred years. The Library is now constructing a plant capable of stabilizing 500,000 volumes a year in this manner.

It may yet prove that the computer is the ultimate savior. The theory behind the entertainment videodisc—laser scanners and digital blips—may be the solution. If books can be scanned and stored digitally on optical disks (as they are in small detail via videodisc and videotape), not only will the preservation problem be resolved, but the great *bulk,* the *mass* of library storage will be compressed. The device will tie the reader to a television tube or a printer, but the contents of the original piece—be it a color film motion picture, a medieval manuscript, or a handwritten operatic score—will at least be *somewhere.* In our present mode, paper-supported scientific data are turning to flakes faster than the library world at large can save them.

The Library's preservationists think they see the first firm light at the end of a tunnel that has worried the profession for a century.

Such preservation, of course, does indeed relate to mass data and its target is books by the thousands. The Library's preservation unit also deals in single items—rare incunabula, individual vellum sheets, and one-of-a-kind Civil War photographs. These are lovingly repaired with infinite care, as precious artifacts. As the rows of antique bindings are carefully oiled, the preservationists are acutely aware of their responsibility to scholars generations into the future.

IN SUMMARY, THEN, JUST WHAT IS THE LIBRARY OF CONGRESS?

One of the most graceful answers to this question was given in 1975 by Senator Howard W. Cannon, then the Chairman of the Committee on Rules and Administration, as he looked back on his seventeen years in the Senate.

He said, "Since its establishment on April 24, 1800, the Library of Congress has been an arm of the legislative branch. Even though it is recognized worldwide as the de facto national library of the United States, its primary purpose is and always has been as a reference and research service for the Congress.

"As the chairman or vice-chairman and a member of the Joint Committee on the Library for years, it has been an interesting experience for me to participate in the growth of what historian Allan Nevins calls 'the most broadly useful library on the face of the globe.' It is a library whose single most important expansion was the 1815 purchase of former President Thomas Jefferson's private library to replace the books that our British foes of that day burned in 1814 when they occupied the Capitol Building.

"It was Jefferson himself who used a phrase, which to this day, justifies the comprehensive collecting policy. He said:

I do not know that my library contains any branch of science which Congress would wish to exclude from their collection: there is, in fact, no subject to which a Member of Congress may not have occasion to refer.

"One unique aspect of the Library's work, at issue in certain quarters, is the dual nature of its services, namely, as legislative library for the Congress, and as a national library for the general public, the professional library community, the executive agencies of the Federal Government, plus scholars, historians, and scientists from around the world. This combination has benefited everyone."

The Reading Rooms

IF YOU have come to use the facilities of the Library of Congress—and not just admire the art and architecture of the buildings or peruse the current exhibit—you will be pleased to learn that the Library is really a very open and accessible place. Anyone over high school age may use the general reading rooms, and any person with a serious research purpose may work in the special reading rooms. Although the Library is a veritable treasure trove, special permission is not required to gain entry; however, a need must be demonstrated for access to some of its resources. Even high school students may have special permission to use the Library's facilities if they have letters from their school principals specifying exact needs which cannot be met by other libraries.

This final section of the guide will be devoted to the general and specialized reading rooms in the Library of Congress. Days and hours of opening of the nineteen reading rooms discussed here differ somewhat. For information on the particular reading room you are interested in, please refer to the insert which accompanies this guide or call the Library of Congress on (202) 287-6400.

A few guidelines on how to make the most efficient use of the Library's staff and collections, and thus the most efficient use of your time, may be helpful at this point. But first, two facts: The bookstacks in the Library of Congress are closed to the public. You must submit call slips for the materials you want, and they will be delivered to you. And, the books cannot be taken out of the Library. Loan privileges are restricted to official borrowers and other libraries.

Guidelines

First: The Library of Congress is, indeed, the largest library in the world. It follows that the answers to most of your questions can probably be found at LC, somewhere. But in that "somewhere" lies the complication: the vastness and complexity of the Library's collections make it much more difficult to locate any single item. Instead of the two and a half drawers of catalog cards on Shakespeare that you would expect to find in a university library, for example, the Library of Congress has twenty-two trays of cards on that topic. It will, therefore, take longer to pinpoint the specific volumes you think will be useful, and longer still to retrieve them from the shelves. A college or university library, or even a large public library, will undoubtedly have the recent general reference works on Shakespeare and may be able to fulfill all of your research needs much more quickly and easily.

Second: Do whatever general research and preparation you can at your local library, college or public, before coming to the Library of Congress. Then you will have a better idea of your specific research needs and you will be able to concentrate your time at LC on those unique resources which your local library was unable to provide. In other words, come prepared.

Third: Plan your trips to the Library of Congress, if possible, during the summer or midwinter months when the *general* reading rooms are apt to be less busy. Fall and spring are the worst times to come, with the absolute nadir being Thanksgiving weekend, when you will probably have to wait just to find a seat in one of the general reading rooms.

Fourth: If you are using one of the two large *general* reading rooms, find out (by consulting a reference librarian) which of the buildings houses most of the books you wish to use. Then select a desk in the reading room in that building. You will be closer to the books you are drawing on, and they will be delivered to you much more quickly.

Fifth: Plan to spend a reasonable amount of time at the Library of Congress in order to do your research. Even though you come prepared and know precisely what you need, it takes time to get materials from the shelves. The collections are heavily used, especially in current, topical, subject areas, and someone else may be using the volumes you want. Running in for an hour at lunchtime is not going to work!

Sixth: There are a number of other publications about the Library of Congress, its collections, its reading rooms, and its services that you may find helpful. Some of them are free brochures, others are more extensive, priced publications. The pamphlets on the reading rooms and reader facilities are available at the Research Guidance Office, which is located just inside the doors to the Main Reading Room in the Jefferson building. You will particularly want to ask for "Information for Readers in the Library of Congress" and "Tips for Students." The sales shop in the lower lobby of the Jefferson building carries the Library's priced publications. If you have come to the Library to use some of its special collections, *Special Collections in the Library of Congress: A Selective Guide,* compiled by Annette Melville (Library of Congress, 1980), may be of particular interest to you. Other Library publications are listed in the booklet, *Library of Congress Publications in Print,* which is available free at the sales shop.

MAIN READING ROOM

The Main Reading Room in the Library's Thomas Jefferson Building is usually the best place to start your research at the Library of Congress. It is a substantial reference library all by itself, with a 40,000-volume reference collection on all subjects housed in the alcoves around the room. The Main Reading Room and its collections can be thought of as the index to the whole encyclopedia of knowledge that is the Library of Congress. Once you have discovered what resources you need to tap, using the index (or Main Reading Room materials), you can call for the volumes you want from the Library's general collections. Should you wish to move from the general to the more specialized collections, you can then pursue your research in one of the special reading rooms or by consulting one of the Library's resident subject specialists. In fact, you may be able to complete all of your research in one of the general reading rooms.

Reference assistance.   Your first stop in the Main Reading Room should be at the Research Guidance Office. A reference librarian will acquaint you with the resources and facilities of the Main Reading Room, describe the procedures necessary to use it, or, if appropriate, refer you to another facility in the Library. Reference librarians are also stationed at the Central Desk (in the middle of the room), in alcoves 4 and 5 between the first two parts of the card catalog, and at the computer catalog center at the back of the card catalog to the rear of the building. The reading room reference staff can help you find what you need in the card catalogs, answer questions about the reference collection, suggest additional information sources, and provide assistance in the use of the automated data bases.

Catalogs and finding aids.   The general card catalog for the Library's collections is in the Main Reading Room; it occupies portions of two rooms and all of a third. It contains 25 million cards. Readers may also use the terminals in the computer catalog center to access the Library of Congress Computerized Catalog (LCCC) as well as other automated data bases. It is important to remember that the Library's computerized card catalog encompasses only those books published since 1968 (with some exceptions), and that no new catalog *cards* have been filed in the card catalog since January 1981. The two catalog files (card and computerized) must therefore be used in conjunction with one another in order to get a complete picture of the Library's holdings on any given topic. A second point is just as important to keep in mind: not everything in the Library's collections will appear in the main catalog (card or computerized). Many collections are cataloged only in the special reading room which has custody of

A reader in
the Main
Reading
Room

them, and even those may be controlled only in huge chunks (especially the nonbook materials) because of the incredible number of pieces involved. Books converted to microform (either acquired that way as part of a larger collection or converted to a micro format for preservation purposes) may or may not appear in the main catalog. And so on. Do not assume the volume is not in the Library of Congress just because it does not appear as a main entry in the catalog. Check with the reference staff if you have any such questions.

There are other finding aids in the Main Reading Room which may prove useful. *Dissertation Abstracts* will let you know if there are any recent dissertations on your subject; the dissertations themselves are available in microform in the Microform Reading Room. The separate serials catalog may save you a little time. Bound serials (two or three years old at least) must be requested in the general reading rooms; current serials (within the last year or two), which have not yet been bound together, must be requested in the Newspaper and Current Periodical Reading Room. The catalog of the books in the Main Reading Room's reference collection will guide you to those sources more quickly, and the multivolume *National Union Catalog* may help you to locate a book you are unable to find in the main catalog.

A very specialized searching service called the National Referral Center, which provides access not to books and literature but to people and places, is available to users of the general reading rooms. Using the computer terminals you can dip into a memory bank that

A Computer Catalog Center in the Main Reading Room provides a bank of terminals so that readers can search the Library of Congress Computerized Catalog.

contains data on 13,000 organizations working in the major fields of the humanities and the physical, biological, social, and engineering sciences to find out who knows what. They may be able to connect you with someone who is doing research in your very field of interest. The services of the National Referral Center, all free, are also available by telephone and by mail.

Procedures for use. To request the items you need, fill out a call slip for each one and turn the slips in at the Central Desk. You will have to wait from thirty minutes to an hour for the requested materials to be delivered to your seat. If the books are not on the shelf, that fact will be noted on the call slip when it is returned to you. You may request a special search for particular items from the Collections Management staff stationed in alcove 7; in many cases they will be able to locate the book that same day.

Special services. If you need to consult the same books on several successive days, you may reserve up to three volumes for no more than three days at a time. If you are undertaking a major research project and anticipate working with the Library's collections over an extended period of time, you may request a study shelf from the Research Facilities Office in alcove 8. A limited number of study desks are also available under certain circumstances for full-time researchers. Advanced planning is highly recommended. In those rare cases when your research needs cannot be satisfied by general reading room service, you may apply at the Central Desk for a special pass to admit you to the bookstacks.

Self-service, coin-operated copying machines are available for your use in the general reading rooms. The Library's Photoduplication Service can also provide photostats, microfilms, and other photocopies of materials in the Library's collections, subject to copyright and other restrictions, but there is generally a four- to six-week turnaround time on this service. Typewriters and voice recorders may not

"Minerva," Roman goddess of wisdom and symbolic patroness of the Library, as depicted in a mosaic by Elihu Vedder for the Thomas Jefferson Building

NIL INVITA MINERVA QUAE MONUMENTUM
ÆRE PERENNIUS EXEGIT

be used in the general reading rooms, but the head of the Main Reading Room issues permits on a first-come, first-served basis to a very limited area for occasional, short-term use.

SOCIAL SCIENCE READING ROOM

The Social Science Reading Room is located on the fifth floor of the Adams building. Its reference collection focuses primarily on business and economics, political science, education, and sociology. Special areas include Abstracts and Indexes, shelved in call number order along the east wall and on both sides of the adjacent alcove; Biographies, shelved along the rear wall; and the Business and Economics

Ezra Winter's lunette at the end of the Jefferson Reading Room in the John Adams Building represents the prologue to Chaucer's *Canterbury Tales*.

area, containing loose-leaf publications, current journals, selected newspapers, and microfiche, as well as current state and local industrial manuals and directories.

Procedures for use and special services are generally the same as those in the Main Reading Room. Readers may use computer terminals which provide access to the Library's Computerized Catalog for entries cataloged in 1968 or later. There is, however, no card catalog in the Social Science Reading Room. You must use the printed book catalogs available in the central hall adjacent to the reading room; not all items listed in the book catalog are in the Library of Congress. The reference staff is near the front of the room.

MICROFORM READING ROOM

The Microform Reading Room provides readers with a different kind of entrée into the general collections of the Library of Congress—a machine to read microfilm and microfiche. It is a natural extension of the general reading room services of the Library. The microfilm collections have grown over the years as the technology has improved and as the need has increased to store large amounts of materials in less space. As a reader doing research in the Library of Congress, you will probably need to dip into the microform collections at some point in the course of your work, regardless of your subject area.

Procedures for use. You should stop at the desk near the door to sign the daily registration sheet and explain the purpose of your visit to the reference librarian. He or she, in turn, will describe the card catalog and the other finding aids in the reading room and tell you how to request the specific items you want. If you are not familiar with the operation of the reading machines, the attendant will show you how they work. Coin-operated printers, which give you paper copies of individual frames from the microfilm or microfiche (with a choice of enlargements), are also available. The reading room can accommodate thirty-three users. The microform collections are stored on decks near the reading room, and on normal days you can expect delivery of the items you have requested within ten to fifteen minutes.

The collections. The microform collections are enormous—2,662,617 microform units as of January 1985. And they cover a fascinating array of topics. Some of the collections were acquired by the Library as a unit (U.S. city directories to 1901, American fiction 1774-1905), and others come in on a regular basis (doctoral dissertations, U.S. corporation annual reports, Foreign Broadcast Information Service daily reports). Many hundreds of monographs and serials from the Library's regular collections are added each year as they are filmed for preservation purposes. Some other examples of the collections found in the Microform Reading Room are: early American imprints; witness index to U.S. congressional hearings; state labor reports 1865-1900; eighteenth- and nineteenth-century American architectural books; collections of pamphlets, broadsides and serials on American history, women's rights 1814-1912, the Shaker movement, and right wing organizations; English and American plays 1516-1830; English parish registers sixteenth to nineteenth centuries; minutes of the Senate of the Venetian Republic; archives of the Austrian Foreign Office 1848-1918; early Latin American imprints;

Patron using a microfilm reader

78

sixteenth- and seventeenth-century Russian imprints; archives of the Japanese Ministry of Foreign Affairs and other ministries 1868-1945; and U.N. documents.

Catalogs and finding aids. A card catalog in the Microform Reading Room provides access to some of the materials in the custody of the section, and other collections can be found through the use of individual printed guides. An important point to remember is that the Library's Central Charge File is annotated to indicate whenever a volume in the general collections is removed from circulation because of its poor condition, filmed, and sent to the Microform Reading Room for use by readers. This change is only reflected in the Library's main card catalog as the last step in the process.

Special services. You may keep materials you are using on reserve in the reading room so that you will not have to request them anew each day. You may also use typewriters and voice recorders, as long as they do not disturb other readers.

LOCAL HISTORY AND GENEALOGY READING ROOM

The services of this reading room are directed toward readers with an interest in the history of American communities and the people who lived in them. The reference staff helps readers identify publications that relate to the subjects of their research, but the Library staff cannot undertake research in family history or heraldry on behalf of a reader. You should know that the sources at the Library of Congress are largely secondary: e.g., published genealogies, local histories, and genealogical compendiums. If you want to consult primary records and documents, you will need to go to the National Archives. The Local History and Genealogy Reading Room will one day house a new American Division, which will have as its focus American history and letters.

Procedures for use. If you have come to the Library of Congress to do some research into your family history, the reference specialists suggest that you read at least one book on the subject of genealogical research before beginning your search at LC. It will allow you to make better use of your time. The operational procedures in the Local History and Genealogy Reading Room are similar to those in the two large general reading rooms. Submit call slips for the items you want, and they will be delivered to your desk. Any books in the Library's general collections can be brought to you in the LH&G Reading Room.

The collections. Local history and genealogy materials are part of the Library's general collections. In addition, the LH&G Reading

A large heraldry chart on the wall of the Local History and Genealogy Reading Room shows the lineage of George Washington.

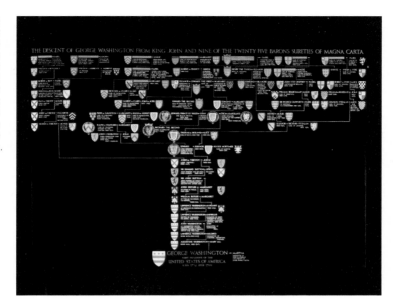

Room maintains a 10,000-volume reference collection to help guide readers to the information sources they need.

Catalogs and finding aids. There are a number of special card catalogs in the reading room that may aid your search. For example, the Family Name Index is a card file for the published genealogies in the Library of Congress, the Analyzed Surname Index provides a guide to genealogical and biographical material found in selected books, and the U.S. Local History Shelflist offers a subject approach to the books dealing with the local history of the states of the United States and their subdivisions (towns, cities, and counties). Published reference aids to genealogical research, such as *Passenger and Immigration Lists Index,* Rider's *American Genealogical-Biographical Index, New England Historical and Genealogical Register,* Swem's *Virginia Historical Index,* and *American and British Genealogy and Heraldry,* can be found in the reading room's reference collection.

Special services. Self-service, coin-operated copiers are available in the reading room. Books may be held on reserve under the same rules that apply to the general reading rooms. Microfilm and microfiche readers are available for viewing genealogical collections in microformat which are housed in the reading room.

NEWSPAPER AND
CURRENT PERIODICAL READING ROOM

The Newspaper and Current Periodical Reading Room is part of the Serial and Government Publications Division, which maintains the largest collection of newspapers, unbound periodicals, and serially issued government publications in the United States. Current receipts of domestic and foreign newspapers total some seventeen hundred titles. Back files of many of these titles are on microfilm, and the reading room has a number of reading machines and printers for readers to use. You will want to visit this reading room to use current, unbound periodicals, such as *Science* or the *American Journal of Agricultural Economics,* as well as the newspapers. You may use the bound volumes of periodicals in one of the general reading rooms. Students who are working with recent U.S. government publications should start their research in the Newspaper and Current Periodical Reading Room, because the reference and bibliographic services provided there will make their task a good deal easier.

Procedures for use. If you are a first-time user of the reading room, you should confer with the staff at the central desk to familiarize yourself with the room's services and facilities. You will find two different forms for requesting materials: one for serials and government publications, the other for newspapers. The decks are closed to the public, but, except in the most unusual circumstances, you can expect delivery of the items you request within a half hour. Five of the most frequently used newspapers—the *Washington Post,* the *Washington Star,* the *New York Times,* the *London Times,* and the *Wall Street Journal*—are stored on microfilm in cabinets in the reading room. You may retrieve these volumes for yourself.

Many of the newspaper titles in the Library's collections are on microfilm

The collections. In addition to its current receipts of newspapers, the division has extensive holdings in eighteenth-, nineteenth-, and twentieth-century newspapers, both foreign and domestic. Its serial and unbound periodicals collection numbers approximately two million pieces. Newspapers and periodicals in Oriental languages are in the custody of the Asian and the African and Middle Eastern Divisions. Current serials and newspapers in Slavic and Baltic languages are available through the European Reading Room. Two of the special collections in the division's custody are the Pulp Fiction Collection (popular American fiction magazines that specialized in science fiction, adventure, romance, and sports—dating from the 1920s to the 1950s) and the Comic Book Collection (2,700 titles, 68,500 pieces), which have come into the Library through the copyright deposit. The latter covers the full range of comic book subject matter: western, science fiction, detective, adventure, war, romance, horror, and humor. It is most comprehensive from 1950 to the present. Because of the rapid deterioration of the paper, however, this particular collection is available only to those readers who are engaged in serious research.

Catalogs and finding aids. Periodicals and government publications held in the division are listed by title in the card catalog in the reading room. Newspaper holdings can be determined by using a variety of bibliographic tools, and the reading room's reference collection will help guide the reader to other sources of information. Brochures, bibliographies, and other finding aids are prepared by the division to describe its collections; one of these is *Newspapers Currently Received in the Library of Congress,* now in its ninth edition.

Special services. Coin-operated printers and photocopying machines are available in the reading room. Materials may be held on reserve for a period of three days, and readers may use their own typewriters and voice recorders in the reading room.

SCIENCE READING ROOM

Although one normally thinks of literature, history, and the arts when considering the strengths of the collections in the Library of Congress, in fact, its scientific holdings are extraordinarily strong. What is more, they have always been so. Few libraries could match Thomas Jefferson's collection of eighteenth-century experimental records when they arrived at the Library in 1815. And once Librarian Ainsworth Rand Spofford made an agreement with Secretary of the Smithsonian Joseph Henry in 1866 to accept at the Library of Congress the scientific volumes that had been pouring into the Smithsonian Institution as a result of exchanges with nations and organizations around the world, the Library's collections in scientific areas could not be approached. The Library of Congress continues to collect works on all aspects of science and technology, with the exception of technical agriculture and clinical medicine—which are the provinces of our other two national libraries, the National Agricultural Library and the National Library of Medicine.

Scientific materials are part of the general collections of the Library of Congress, and a separate unit to provide a central focus for science and technology was not created in the Library until after World War II and the postwar boom in scientific research. That unit evolved into today's Science and Technology Division, which operates a Science Reading Room to provide reference services to users of

The Library of Congress has been preparing comprehensive bibliographies on cold regions for some three decades. This National Science Foundation photograph shows the Meserve Glacier in Antarctica.

the Library's science and technology collections. If your research at the Library of Congress is related to a scientific or technological field, you will want to start your quest in the Science Reading Room.

Procedures for use. Upon entering the Science Reading Room, you will receive an information sheet from the reference librarian giving the location of the different categories of reference materials and explaining how to use the reading room. The reference staff will help to facilitate your search and assist in your use of the reading room reference collection. Some of the materials you will want to use may be located right in the reading room. Sixty percent of the Library's extensive collection of technical reports (which includes reports issued by the Department of Energy, the National Aeronautics and Space Administration, the Department of Defense, and other U.S. government agencies), for example, are in the custody of the Science and Technology Division. Most of these are on microfiche and can be examined using the microfiche readers adjacent to the reading room. In addition, vertical files, containing pamphlets, journal articles, and bibliographies on a wide variety of scientific and technological topics of current interest are available for general reader use. You can request other materials from the general collections or from the division's special collections.

The collections. The Library's science and technology collections number some three million volumes, nearly sixty thousand journals (forty thousand current titles) and 3.2 million technical reports. The reference collection in the Science Reading Room includes technical dictionaries, encyclopedias, handbooks, directories, and standard reference texts in the basic sciences, as well as current issues of selected science journals and major abstracting and indexing journals in the physical, earth, biomedical, and engineering sciences. The collections, which are especially strong in aeronautical materials, include such treasures as first editions of Copernicus and Newton and the personal papers of the Wright Brothers and Alexander Graham Bell.

Catalogs and finding aids. Computer terminals in the Science Reading Room provide the principal access to the Library's general collections. Book catalogs for pre-1968 materials are located in an adjacent hallway. A number of special scientific finding aids, such as abstracting and indexing journals, are part of the division's reference collection.

Special services. The Science and Technology Division prepares an informal series of reference guides, called "Tracer Bullets," which are targeted to the literature of a given topic (such as alcohol fuels, edible wild plants, genetic engineering, or acid rain). Each of these guides is designed to direct you to the essential information you will need by listing the basic texts, reports, conference proceedings, government publications, and journal articles on that particular subject. The individual "Tracer Bullets" as well as a complete listing of the whole series are available free upon request. More extensive bibliographies, such as their *Wilbur & Orville Wright: A Chronology Commemorating the Hundredth Anniversary of the Birth of Orville Wright, August 19, 1871,* are published from time to time. Coin-operated copying machines, as well as microfiche printers, are accessible in and near the Science Reading Room. Books may be held on reserve for up to three days.

LAW LIBRARY READING ROOM

The Law Library is the oldest department in the Library of Congress. It was established by the Congress in 1832 as a separate "apartment near to, and connected by an easy communication with that in which the Library of Congress is now kept." This very separation actually saved many of the oldest books in the Law Library from destruction, when two-thirds of the rest of the Library's collections burned in a fire in the Capitol in 1851. The Law Library opened with 2,011 volumes in 1832, 639 of which had been in Thomas Jefferson's private library. Today it contains 1.9 million volumes, including the world's largest and most comprehensive collection of foreign, international, and comparative law. Its strength lies equally in its human resources. In addition to American law librarians, foreign legal specialists with knowledge of more than fifty languages provide reference and research service in all known legal systems.

The Law Library is in a unique situation in the Library of Congress. Like the Congressional Research Service, its primary responsibility is to provide research and reference assistance to the Congress. Unlike CRS, however, the Law Library also serves the U.S. federal courts, executive branch agencies of the government, members of the bench and bar, research organizations, those concerned with legal scholarship, and the general public. Congress calls upon the Law Library principally for its expertise in foreign law and legal systems, including common law, civil law, Roman law, canon law, Chinese law, Jewish law, Islamic law, and ancient and medieval law. The Law Library prepared approximately 1,100 studies for the Congress in 1984 and explored how foreign governments applied the law to solve their particular social or political problems. Congress may also call upon the Law Library for reference assistance in American law, by mail, by phone, or in person in the main Law Library or through the 30,000-volume library the Law Library maintains in the Capitol (which is required by statute to remain open and available to members of Congress and their staffs whenever the House or the Senate is in session). The bulk of American law reference and in-depth research in American law, however, is provided to the Congress by the American Law Division of the Congressional Research Service.

The Law Library was the second major public reading room to open in the Library's James Madison Memorial Building. Its current reader facilities are much improved over those in its old quarters in the Jefferson building, with seats for 176 readers and a veiw of the atrium garden through floor to ceiling glass walls.

Procedures for use. If you have come to use the resources of the Law Library, you will find that it is organized much like other large law libraries you may have used. The Law Library concentrates on collecting all legal materials, such as constitutions, codes and compilations of laws, official gazettes, court decisions, session laws, administrative rules and treatises and decisions, from U.S. jurisdictions as well as from around the world. Many of these resources will be found in the reading room's reference collection, along with recent issues of the major legal periodicals and federal legislative materials (reports, committee prints, bills, resolutions, and documents). The materials on the open shelves of the reading room are generally

The Law Library has a separate area for its collection of rare books

available for immediate use by you as a reader. You should request other volumes from the Law Library's closed stack collection (shelved four floors below) by using the request forms available in the reading room and turning them in at the circulation desk. Materials brought up from the stacks are delivered to the circulation desk; they are not delivered to the individual readers at the study tables. The wait for delivery of books from the stacks is normally about 45 minutes to one hour.

Reference librarians will help you to find what you need in the Library's catalogs or explain the use of the computer terminals. Although the terminals also provide access to the Library of Congress Computerized Catalog, books from the Library's general collections cannot be delivered to the Law Library (and vice versa).

The collections. The Law Library's 1.9 million-volume collection is 45 percent American, 55 percent foreign law. It is known in legal circles for the depth and breadth of its collections from other nations around the globe, as well as for its extraordinarily comprehensive U.S. holdings. Its collection of U.S. legislative documents— from 1789 to the present—is heavily used. The Law Library's complete set of U.S. Supreme Court records and briefs and its collection of U.S. Courts of Appeals records and briefs are invaluable to practicing members of the bar. The Law Library has a separate Rare Book facility, located adjacent to the reading room, which contains such holdings as the early editions of the laws of American states and territories, the *Coutume* Collection (compilations of French customary legal sources, some dating back to the fifteenth century and magnificently illuminated by hand), as well as large holdings of Roman and canon law, and unique manuscripts and incunabula.

Catalogs and finding aids. All of the traditional legal finding tools are in the Law Library Reading Room, as well as an extensive card catalog for the monograph collections. This is particularly useful for works in English published before 1968, and for most of the foreign law collections. Since 1968, legal volumes, like other books in the Library's collections, have been included in the computerized catalog and bibliographic data for them are accessible on-line via the computer terminals.

Special services. Coin-operated copying machines and microfilm and microfiche reader-printers are available in the reading room. A separate briefing room is available for those using typewriters or recording equipment. Books may be reserved in the reading room for up to three days, and serious legal scholars may obtain stack passes as well as study desks in the subbasement.

PERFORMING ARTS

The nonbook collections of the Library of Congress in the performing arts areas—music, dance, sound recordings, motion pictures, and television—developed and expanded independently over the years. Many of the different formats had their own reading room areas, often unrelated to the others. Researchers studying one aspect of performing arts like musical comedy, for example, would have to move from one place to another in order to examine all of the materials at the Library relevant to their topic.

With the opening of the new James Madison Memorial Building, an opportunity to create a new entity, a Performing Arts Reading Room, has become a reality. In this facility, the user has access to music manuscripts, videotapes, and recorded discs and cassettes; the subject of the research is king, not the format of the material.

Reference service is provided by specialists stationed at the central desk in the Performing Arts Reading Room. In addition, the Recorded Sound Reference Center, located at the south end of the reading room, assists users who are primarily interested in sound recordings and radio materials. It houses the Library of Congress printed card catalog for sound recordings and a card index for many of the Library's uncataloged recordings. Specialized indexes and reference materials are also located there.

Listening facilities are available in the Performing Arts Reading Room without charge, but their use is limited to persons doing research of a specific nature leading to publication or production.

The music collections of the Library represent a classic example of a complete library within a library. They consist of books about music, the nearly seven million pieces of sheet music spanning the history of music in America from the eighteenth century to yesterday's copyright deposits, complete individual collections like 12,500 opera librettos collected by a single man, and, of course, the rarities of manuscript materials and musical instruments.

Procedures for use. Notwithstanding that so much of the collection is unbound music, as a visitor to the new reading room, you can relate to it in the same manner as you would to your hometown book library. If you are familar with the public finding aids and know what you want, you can go to the numerous catalogs, some of which are described below, find the title you wish, fill out a call slip in the same manner as you would for a book, and present the slip at the service desk. An attendant will go into the stacks and bring the material to you and you can use it either at the study tables in the reading room

In 1951 the noted violinist Fritz Kreisler gave the Library his Guarnerius, his Hill bow, and the autograph manuscript of the Brahms Violin Concerto.

or, if you wish to read the music at a piano, you can request the use of the soundproof room equipped for score reading.

In most cases, you will be best served if you go directly to the reference desk and explain your purpose. A desk attendant or a music specialist can usually chart a direct and efficient approach to your problem. The music stacks are closed, browsing is not permitted, and the collections are so extensive and complex that it is wise to explain your needs at the desk before attempting to locate the finding aids you need by yourself.

The collections. The Library's musical collections are without peer in many areas. For example, opera, musical comedy, motion picture scores, and ballet music are extensively represented. The copyright deposits contain the most comprehensive collection of popular music anywhere in the world. The Music Division also has unique manuscript scores of, among others, Bach, Brahms, Beethoven, Liszt, Mozart, Mendelssohn, and Schoenberg, revealing the successive changes in composition which led to the masterpieces that have become a part of our musical heritage. And the Library's collections of *American* composers in manuscript exceed any institution's anywhere.

The music collection's user audience is as broad as any unit's in the Library. Musicologists, motion picture producers, performing artists, composers, and students of popular culture all come to explore the millions of pieces of material.

Catalogs and finding aids. The visitor will find numerous card catalogs housed in a typical catalog bank at the north end of the reading room. There are basically four areas:

The first catalog contains entries for *books about music.* It is arranged by author, title, and subject in the traditional manner of a dictionary catalog.

The second catalog is a specialized one, containing material on music theory and teaching, exclusively. It is also arranged in the author, title, subject manner.

The third catalog indexes the Library's enormous collection of opera librettos, including all those acquired through copyright plus the comprehensive acquisitions that have come from abroad through most of the twentieth century. But do not think *all* the librettos are in this catalog. The more than 12,500 librettos in the Schatz Collection referred to earlier are in a separate index!

The fourth catalog is both the most useful and the most unusual. It is limited to music—notes, as they appear in sheet music, collections, and complete scores. This catalog is in turn divided into three parts. One part is filed by composer, the second part is filed by title, and the third part is filed by call number: a *classed* catalog.

The advantage of this classed catalog is that it gathers music together by *kind.* Thus, if the reader wants carols, harpsichord solos, Moog transcriptions, harpsichord, flute, and cello trios, these will be sorted so that similar songs are filed together. This permits the browsing that would normally take place in open shelves. So, if a reader is looking for Mexican music, songs about Duke University, drum and bagpipe music, or piano music to accompany silent motion pictures, each of these is a discrete subject classification and can be examined a card at a time, in sequence. The librarians repeatedly plead, however: if you do not find what you want in the catalog, do not assume it does not exist. Less than a third of the Music Division's holdings are cataloged. Ask the music specialist. He or she may know of a shortcut that will take you directly to your target.

Special services. The Library's greatest pride in the music collections comes from the one-of-a-kind manuscripts that cover the entire span of Western music. Since so many of these rest in enormous collections of unpublished materials, scribbled notes, notebooks, and letter files (for example, the Library has the Sergei Rachmaninoff archives, as well as the musical manuscripts of Richard Rodgers and John Philip Sousa), the best approach to this material is via conferences with the appropriate curator of materials.

The Performing Arts Reading Room is the public entrée to the Music Division which not only provides and cares for the musical materials, but also produces the Library's concerts; cares for the Stradivari, Guarnerius, and Amati stringed instruments and the collection of over sixteen hundred flutes in the Miller Collection; and commissions the many new compositions the Library receives and performs under the auspices of the several foundations established in the division for such activities. The division also accepts inquiries by correspondence; after a scholar has exhausted the resources of his home community, he may write the Library for reference assistance.

PERFORMING ARTS LIBRARY
AT THE KENNEDY CENTER

Visitors to the roof terrace level of the John F. Kennedy Center for the Performing Arts may be a little startled to find an outpost of the Library of Congress nestled at the east end of the north gallery. A joint project of the Library of Congress and the Kennedy Center, the Performing Arts Library serves two purposes: it provides artists and designers working at the Kennedy Center access to the basic research tools of their craft, and it offers performers and visitors alike a window into the much more extensive collections in the performing arts located at the Library of Congress. The reading room is open to the public and can accommodate forty-four readers. Exhibit cases and panels around the room display items from the collections of the Library and the Kennedy Center, and the changing exhibits are designed to appeal to the interested visitor as well as to the more serious scholar of the performing arts.

Procedures for use. The reading room reference librarians specialize in various aspects of the perfoming arts, and they are well equipped to put you in touch with the resources you may need— whether those resources are in the collections at the Library of Congress or in another performing arts collection elsewhere in the United States. The Library of Congress Computerized Catalog is accessible via a terminal with a video display screen, and a remote audio link allows users to listen by appointment to sound recordings relayed directly from the Library of Congress.

The collections. The Performing Arts Library brings together reference works on music, dance, theater, film, and broadcasting in its 5,000-volume collection housed in the reading room. It also has over 375 current periodicals, the 2,800-disc White House Record Library, videotapes, posters and an extensive vertical file. Readers may view materials from the Kennedy Center Archives in the library by prior arrangement.

The complete collections of the Performing Arts Library are potentially all of the collections in the performing arts at the Library of Congress and the Kennedy Center. The Library's collections are spelled out in greater detail in the sections of this guide describing the individual reading rooms at the Library of Congress where the different collections may be used. But a quick summary will give you an idea of the extent of the performing arts materials you can draw on: from Manuscript, personal papers of notable personalities associated with films and the theater, and radio and dramatic scripts; from Motion Picture, films covering the whole history of motion pictures, television films and videotapes, and sound recordings; from Music, books and periodicals on all aspects of musical activity, instructional literature in music, manuscript scores, letters and scrap books of composers, and printed music; from Prints and Photographs, portraits of performers, drawings and architectural plans of American theaters, and theatrical posters; and from Rare Book, English and American playbills, selected copyright manuscript plays, theater broadsides, and early printed books on theater and dance. All of these are, of course, in addition to the performing arts volumes contained in the Library's general and newspaper and periodical collections.

Catalogs and finding aids. In addition to the card catalog for its reference collection, there is a computer terminal in the Performing Arts Library Reading Room which gives readers access to the Library of Congress Computerized Catalog for most books published since 1968. There are also a number of specialized indexes and finding aids in the reference collection. Because of the nature of the Performing Arts Library, however, you may need to rely heavily on the expertise and experience of the reference librarians, who can either help you to find the particular item you need or guide you in the use of the more extensive catalogs in the various specialized collections at the Library of Congress or the Kennedy Center Archives.

Special services. In addition to the unique links to the Library of Congress collections already mentioned, there are individual listening and viewing stations next to the reading room. The Performing Arts Library also has a conference room which is available by appointment for group listening and viewing and for library-related meetings and seminars. A copying machine and a microform reader-printer are located in the reading room.

MOTION PICTURE, BROADCASTING, AND RECORDED SOUND READING ROOMS

The Library of Congress's collection of films and recorded sound materials started with the earliest examples of the art, and it changed and developed through the years as the technology evolved. In order to protect their innovative creations, the first moviemakers wanted to register their moving pictures with the Copyright Office. Since there was no provision in the copyright law applicable to pictures that moved, the early films were registered and deposited as photographs printed on rolls of paper. They became known as the Paper Print Collection. Modern technology has now permitted these early paper prints of motion pictures to be rephotographed and converted back into actual films. Some three thousand have been restored through this process. Today, the library's film and television collections contain more than one hundred thousand titles, with several thousand new ones being added each year through copyright deposit, purchase, gift, or exchange.

The recorded sound collection also traces its origins back to the beginning of this century, when a Yale professor by the name of E. W. Scripture made a wax cylinder recording of the voice of Kaiser Wil-

Readers can make arrangements to view films from the Library's collections.

helm II of Germany and gave it to the Library of Congress. In 1924, the Victor Talking Machine Company, in the interest of archival preservation, began to deposit a selection of its phonograph records in the Library. Rival companies soon followed suit, and the Library began to acquire sound recordings in earnest. Today's recorded sound collections include over 1.3 million recordings of music and spoken word from about 1890 to the present. They are contained on a variety of recording formats, including cylinders, discs, piano rolls, magnetic wires, and magnetic tapes. Noncommercial material makes up about 60 percent of the collection—American radio broadcasts, original field recordings of ethnographic interest, recordings of the Library's music and literary programs, and unpublished materials acquired from private collectors. The commercial sound holdings are predominately American, although the collections are international in scope.

Procedures for use.　The film, television, and recorded sound collections of the Library of Congress are maintained for research purposes. They are not open to high school students. The film and television collections may only be used by undergraduate college students with a supporting letter from a supervising professor. The collections are not available for public projection, loan, or rental, although copies of individual items may be made under certain circumstances. Separate viewing and listening facilities for individual readers are provided in the reading rooms, but, except for recorded sound, they must be scheduled well in advance because space is limited.

Two separate reading facilities are maintained—one for motion pictures and television, and the other for broadcasting and recorded sound. You should discuss your specific needs with the reference specialists in each of the two areas so that they can advise you how to proceed.

The collections—motion pictures.　The Library has an unusually strong collection of films produced before 1915, including those that have been restored from the Paper Print Collection. The Theodore Roosevelt Collection of 380 titles, which is especially valuable for revealing the political and social history of the early twentieth century; the George Kleine Collection of 456 titles from the first decades of the film industry; and the more than 700 early titles in the American Film Institute Collection are some of them.

Although the copyright law was amended in 1912 to cover motion pictures, the Library of Congress decided not to accept the film deposits themselves because of the danger in handling the unstable nitrate film used at the time. This situation prevailed until 1942 when

The Library's Recording Laboratory has both archival and preservation responsibilities.

the importance of films as an historical record tipped the balance in favor of resuming their collection. When the American Film Institute was established in 1967, therefore, it was not surprising that they decided to concentrate some of their efforts on recovering films produced between 1912 and 1942, the years for which the Library of Congress had retained only descriptive material relating to the films. A cooperative agreement between LC and AFI has resulted in the deposit of all films acquired by the American Film Institute in the Library of Congress.

Films by all American studios are represented in the Library's collections, and an active preservation effort is making great strides at converting the Library's nitrate films to acetate safety film so that they can be viewed by researchers. The motion picture collections also include several thousand films produced in Germany, Japan, and Italy between 1930 and 1945. U.S.-government-produced films, like other government records, are in the custody of the National Archives.

The collections—television. In 1949 the Library began to collect films made for television as part of their motion picture collections. Many copyrighted television programs are now being deposited on film and videotape. The 1976 copyright law revision created in the Library of Congress a new American Television and Radio Archives, which in the future will provide the focus for a greater emphasis on television as a separate entertainment form.

The collections—recorded sound. Until 1972, the Library's collections of recorded sound materials were acquired by gift, exchange, or purchase. With the change in the copyright law of that year to include recordings under its protection, many new commercial records began to come to the Library through copyright. The collection, some 1.3 million items, covers the whole history of sound recordings, from wax cylinders to compact audio discs.

Some of the collections of unusual historic interest are the Berliner Collection, a selection of papers and recordings representing Emile Berliner, who invented and introduced the disc recording; the Joel Berger Collection of rare operatic records from prerevolutionary Russia; the John Secrist Collection comprising 2,800 commercial classical music releases from 1902 to 1925; the Raymond Swing Collection of several hundred radio news commentaries broadcast between 1941 and 1946 by one of the most influential newsmen of the period; the Office of War Information Collection, which represents the broadcasts of the OWI from 1942 to 1945; and the Museum of Broadcasting-National Broadcasting Company Collection which covers the period from 1933 to 1970.

Catalogs and finding aids. The division has a small reference collection of books, distributors' catalogs, yearbooks, reviews, trade periodicals, film stills, and descriptive material for films registered for copyright after 1912. The principal access tool to films and videotapes is the alphabetical title catalog in the reading room. The division has also published descriptive guides to some portions of the collections, such as *The George Kleine Collection of Early Motion Pictures in the Library of Congress.* And the Copyright Office's semiannual *Catalog of Copyright Entries: Motion Pictures,* which lists all such materials registered for copyright in the United States, is a useful tool in motion picture research.

A printed card catalog for sound recordings is available and additional finding aids can be used by researchers in the Recorded Sound Reference Center. *The Catalog of Copyright Entries: Sound Recordings* lists sound recordings registered for copyright since 1972.

Special services. The division's Recording Laboratory will tape copies of sound recordings in good physical condition from the collections if written authorization is obtained from proprietary rights holders. A number of recordings from the collections of folk songs, music, and poetry and other literature are available for sale by mail or from the Library's sales shop. Copies of films may also be ordered through the division, under the same conditions and restrictions as sound recordings.

ARCHIVE OF FOLK CULTURE
READING ROOM

In 1928 four private citizens gave the Library of Congress $1,000 apiece to capture authentic American folk music before it was lost forever. Over the next ten years, Library of Congress employees set out with their cumbersome recording machines to collect samples of American folk music from different regions of the United States and bring them back to the Library. Thus, the Archive of Folk Song was born.

The American Folklife Center was created in the Library of Congress in 1976 for the purpose of acting as a central clearinghouse and developing programs that touch and illuminate the varieties of folk cultural traditions in the United States. In 1978, the Archive (renamed the Archive of Folk Culture) joined forces with the American Folklife Center to provide a single focus for folklife research at the Library of Congress. The American Folklife Center is essentially an administrative and research entity, but the fruits of its surveys and field research are accessible through the reading room of the Archive of Folk Culture.

Procedures for use. The Archive of Folk Culture maintains its own listening facility and reading room, and it has continued to do so even after the opening of the Performing Arts Reading Room. However, an audio link between the two facilities is planned for the future. If your research interest centers on folk music, folk culture, ethnomusicology, or grass-roots oral history, whether American or international, you should visit the Archive Reading Room for assistance. Limited listening facilities are available; it is best to make arrangements to use them in advance.

The collections. The Archive controls the largest repository of traditional folklife documentation in the United States, including more than three hundred thousand recorded specimens of songs, instrumental tunes, spoken tales, and other lore from all over the world. It continues to acquire original materials for the Library's collections, in all documentary and printed formats. Although the Archive originally concerned itself with American traditions, its collections today are truly international in scope, covering the music and folk cultural traditions of many nations. The Archive's holdings also include many thousands of pieces of manuscript material.

Catalogs and finding aids. Two card catalogs in the Archive Reading Room will help you to locate the materials you need. One provides a sequential list of recorded collections, with additional access provided through the use of key words such as state names, collectors, featured performers, instruments, language, major genres, and ethnic groups. The other, covering recordings added to the Library's holdings from 1928 to 1950, provides access to each item (such as, tale, song, sermon, tune, or game) on the recording. Additional card indexes will help guide you to manuscripts and microforms on folk culture and ethnomusicology that are located in the Archive and in other custodial units in the Library. Finally, a number of general bibliographies and directories, as well as finding aids to particular parts of the Archive's collections, have been prepared to assist scholars in the field.

Special services.   The Archive operates an intern program to give students in folklore and ethnomusicology experience in all phases of the Archive's activities. During the summer free lunchtime folk concerts are held on the plaza in front of the Thomas Jefferson Building, and the American Folklife Center sponsors regular folk-related programs during the winter months as well. Copies of recorded materials in the Archive's collections may be purchased through the Recording Laboratory of the Motion Picture, Broadcasting, and Recorded Sound Division; in many cases permission must be obtained from proprietary rights holders. The Archive staff will help you make these arrangements. Some eighty-five LP folk recordings are available for sale by mail and at the Library's sales shop. Readers in the Archive Reading Room have access to microfilm and microfiche readers and to a photocopying machine.

John R. Griffin of Lenox, Georgia, demonstrates the technique of fiddle beating for the head of the American Folklife Center

PRINTS AND PHOTOGRAPHS
READING ROOM

Images are captured by the Prints and Photographs Division—in photographs, architectural plans, posters, fine prints, cartoons, drawings, advertising labels, and commercial art. These varied and diverse collections, more than ten million items, may be used by researchers in the Prints and Photographs Reading Room. And they are heavily used: by writers and editors looking for pictures to illustrate their books, by television journalists searching out visuals for the six o'clock news, by art historians tracing the development of a particular print medium, by preservationists seeking to restore a long demolished building, by set designers trying to recreate a nineteenth-century interior design, and so on. The uses for these extensive collections are as creative and diverse as the materials themselves.

From its earliest days, the Library of Congress has collected pictorial materials, initially in the form of book decoration and illustration. In 1898 the gift of 2,700 fine prints and other items by Mrs. Gardiner Greene Hubbard created the impetus for establishing a separate Division of Prints in 1900 to care for these materials. With the accession of huge collections of photographic prints and negatives (now amounting to approximately 90 percent of the division's collections) over the next half-a-century, the nature of the division's collections changed. In recognition of that fact, the division was renamed the Prints and Photographs Division in 1944. Other major gifts, copyright deposits, transfers, exchanges, and purchases have enlarged the collections to their current size and scope.

Procedures for use.   You will be asked to sign a register, noting the purpose of your visit, when you arrive at the Prints and Photographs Reading Room. To protect the materials in the collections, you will also be asked to take notes with a pencil and not a ball-point or wet ink pen. Reference librarians are available to help guide your search of the collections. And if your research takes you into some of the lesser known corners of the specialized collections, such as political cartoons or the photographs of Alexander Graham Bell, you may wish to consult with the division curators of these particular collections.

It is important for you to know that the pictorial collections of the Library of Congress are maintained as a research archive; the division does not have the staff to make lengthy searches for particular pictures or to make editorial selections among them. If you cannot visit the reading room in person to make these kinds of choices, the division can provide you with a list of free-lance picture searchers in the Washington, D.C., area who may be able to assist you.

The collections. The collections of the Prints and Photographs Division are huge. Although they are international in scope, they are richest in material relating to the history and culture of the United States. Photographs: the holdings of nine million photographs and negatives, including news photos, portraits, scenic views, and stereographs, comprise one of the finest general historical collections in the world. Its master photograph collection, consisting of 3,500 original images by noted photographers (such as, Roger Fenton, Arnold Genthe, Clarence White, and F. Holland Day), spans the history of photography from early daguerreotypes to contemporary portfolios. Fine prints: the fine print collection consists of 110,000 woodcuts, engravings, etchings, lithographs, and other print media which range in date from the fifteenth century to the present. The Library has an exceptional collection of chiaroscuro woodcuts (mostly from the sixteenth century) and has made a deliberate attempt to collect artists' self-portraits. Popular and applied graphic art: the historical prints in this collection, 40,000 lithographs, engravings, woodcuts, and other original prints, illustrate eighteenth- and nineteenth-century life in America and Europe. Cartoons, packaging labels, and sketches for il-

Drawing of St. Michael's Cathedral, Sitka, Alaska, from the Historic American Buildings Survey

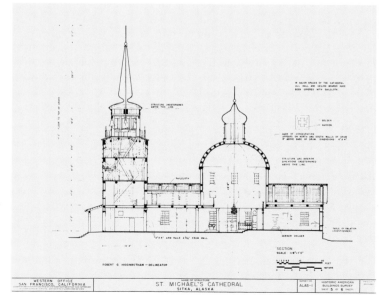

lustrations in American books and magazines add another dimension to our view of everyday life. Architectural drawings: these holdings, numbering more than one hundred thousand items, form the most comprehensive architectural archive in the United States. They include the photographic records of the Historic American Buildings Survey and the Pictorial Archives of Early American Architecture, among others. Posters: war, propaganda, travel, art exhibition, theatrical, and circus posters are represented in this collection of 75,000 American and foreign posters, which range from the 1850s to the present.

Catalogs and finding aids. As you might expect, each of these different kinds of collections has its own special finding aids. There are a number of card catalogs in the reading room that provide access by subject, artist, collector, or publisher. Because of their size, many of the collections are controlled by lot number only so that you may have to leaf through many pieces to find exactly what you want. To facilitate your search, files of photoprint reference copies are maintained by name, subject, or photographer in filing cabinets in the reading room. In addition, many of the printed volumes in the division's reference collections have been annotated to indicate which of the pictures are in the Library's collections.

Special services. Photocopies of materials in the Prints and Photographs Division collections which are not under copyright or other restrictions may be ordered through the Library's Photoduplication Service. Orders usually take four to six weeks to process. Picture searchers are not normally allowed to take photographs of original materials themselves, although some exceptions to this rule can be made. Permission must be requested in advance from the chief of the Prints and Photographs Division. Original materials from the division's collections may be borrowed by institutions that meet certain requirements for display, insurance, and shipping as determined by the Library's Exhibits Office.

MANUSCRIPT READING ROOM

The Manuscript Division was the first of the "treasure" divisions. Its earliest acquisitions were the handwritten records of the Virginia Company of London for the years 1619 to 1625, which were included among the materials Thomas Jefferson sold the Library in 1815. Since then, the manuscripts have grown to over forty million pieces, and the division has become a major repository of the nation's memory.

What are manuscripts? Essentially one-of-a-kind writings which

The Library owns two copies of the Gettysburg Address as written by Abraham Lincoln. It is believed that he held this page in his hand at the dedication of the battlefield.

> **Executive Mansion,**
>
> *Washington,* _____, 186 .
>
> Four score and seven years ago our fathers brought forth, upon this continent, a new nation, conceived in liberty, and dedicated to the proposition that "all men are created equal"
>
> Now we are engaged in a great civil war, testing whether that nation, or any nation so conceived and so dedicated, can long endure. We are met on a great battle field of that war. We have

(according to David Mearns) "possess evidential value, illuminate a personality, or provide a basis for scholarly judgment on actions and events." They may come as letters, diaries, speech drafts, scrapbooks, telegrams, transcribed telephone conversations, or memoranda. These are "the papers of those men and women who, throughout the centuries, have most profoundly influenced the lives and destinies of their countrymen."

Procedures for use. The manuscripts in the collection are almost by definition unique, extraordinarily valuable, and essentially held in trust for the nation; they must therefore be used with care. Most are available, however, to anyone engaged in serious research. When you come to use the materials, you will be asked to register and to present proper identification, preferably with a photograph attached.

Manuscripts are kept by collections (such as the Booker T. Washington papers or the Walt Whitman papers), and there are over ten thousand of these. Since frequently the letters of a notable are actually in the papers of the individual *to whom* he was writing (General McClellan's letters to the president will be in the Lincoln papers), you will wish to consult with the reading room staff before you begin a project.

As you use the collections, the Library requests that you take unusual care that the existing order and arrangement of unbound materials be maintained, that sheets be handled by their margins (to avoid fingerprints and natural oils affecting the handwritten text), and that you use microfilm copies of collections when such editions exist.

The collections. Whose manuscripts are these? They are the writings of an incredible assembly of the individuals who have created the world we live in. The Library owns the papers of twenty-three of the presidents from Washington to Coolidge. It has the personal papers of Clara Barton, Susan B. Anthony, Carrie Chapman Catt, Margaret Sanger, and Clare Boothe Luce. A single aisle, taken at random, contains 175,000 pieces from Sigmund Freud's files and the letters of Lillian Gish, Samuel F. B. Morse, Alexander Graham Bell, Louis Untermeyer, and Daniel Chester French. There are seemingly endless shelves of the revolutionary patriots, Franklin, Jefferson, Hamilton, Morris, and so on.

The Library attempts to acquire the papers of the whole spectrum of American life. American science and technology are represented in the papers of the Wright Brothers, Luther Burbank, Robert Fulton, J. Robert Oppenheimer, and Vannevar Bush. Literary figures, the military, participants in the civil rights movement, women, and representatives of medicine and labor are richly in evidence as well as the more expected political figures.

In addition to the rare manuscripts, since 1905 the division has been accumulating copies of materials in *other* institutions around the world. In the early decades it sent copiers to duplicate by hand materials that bore on the progress of American history. With the development of microfilm copying techniques, photographic technicians have taken the place of the hand copiers, and between the two the division has great quantities of duplicated documents from such depositories as the Archives of the Indies in Seville (which record the Spanish colonization of America), early British colonial reports from the Public Record Office in London, records of the Society for the Propagation of the Gospel (minutely detailed reports sent to England from each parish on the American frontier in the seventeenth and eighteenth centuries), war reports from Hessian officers to their home governments in the Revolution, to cite just a few examples. All of these materials were collected to be used; they are in the division to help American scholarship have a better understanding of our past.

Catalogs and finding aids. Manuscripts are arranged, as a rule, either chronologically by the date they were written or alphabetically by the name of the person who wrote them. While there is no general card catalog or index to all forty million manuscript items in the Library's holdings, descriptions of individual collections of manuscripts are available. For some fifteen hundred or so larger collections, the staff of the Manuscript Division has prepared individual "registers" or typed (and sometimes printed) narrative descriptions which give details about the "provenance" (or source) of the collection; literary rights or copyright interests, when known; biographical information about the principal individuals whose papers are included; the scope and content of the collection; and lists of folder titles, containers, or other descriptions of the manuscripts which are included. For some collections—especially smaller collections and collections of presidential papers—catalogs or indexes of individual manuscript items are available; and, in addition, many subject guides to special fields of research interest have been prepared to help guide readers to rich sources of information in the manuscript holdings.

The Manuscript Division has a professional staff of historians who are available for consultation with visiting researchers. These scholars' specific areas of expertise are as follows: early American history to 1825; the National period to 1861; Civil War and Reconstruction to 1900; twentieth-century political history; cultural and scientific history; and Afro-American history and culture. Appointments can be made at the registration desk for individual consultation with these specialists.

In addition to the catalogs and registers, the Division has special indexes to individual collections; a bound master record which provides current bibliographical data on all the collections; and an inventory, arranged by country, repository, and archival file, of the collection of foreign reproductions. The reading room also maintains a reference collection of materials relating to the individuals and periods represented by the manuscripts in the division's custody.

The Library has prepared published finding aids which, of course, are available in the reading room, but are also commonly in college and public libraries, and you may wish to examine them before coming to Washington. Among these are *National Union Catalog of Manuscript Collections* (annual since 1959); *Manuscripts on Microfilm: A Checklist* (1975); *Manuscript Sources in the Library of Congress for Research in the American Revolution* (1975); and *Members of Congress: A Checklist of Their Papers in the Manuscript Division, Library of Congress* (1980).

Special services. Unbound manuscripts may be photocopied, and there are coin-operated copy machines and microprinters in the reading room. Bound manuscripts can be copied through the Library's Photoduplication Service. Reproductions of manuscripts in foreign repositories and manuscripts on microfilm can usually be borrowed on interlibrary loan, and therefore can be consulted in the researcher's home community. Typewriters, tape recorders, and cameras are permitted.

RARE BOOK AND
SPECIAL COLLECTIONS READING ROOM

The Rare Book and Special Collections Division occupies imposing quarters, modelled after Independence Hall in Philadelphia, on the second floor of the Jefferson building. Entry to the reading room is through two bronze doors, embellished with the printer's marks of such individuals as Johann Fust and Peter Schoeffer, Geoffrey Tory, William Nuthead, and Bruce Rogers, all of whom had a profound influence on the art of printing during their lifetimes.

The identification and protection of "rare books" as a separate category of materials began only about a hundred years ago in the Library of Congress. Bookman-Librarian Ainsworth Rand Spofford began accumulating in his own office those books, pamphlets, broadsides, and printed ephemera known to be of interest to the antiquarian book trade of his day. Many of the older cards in the catalog still carry the designation "Office," denoting an item in the collections deserving special attention, or, quite literally in the late nineteenth century, storage in Spofford's office. As other valuable special collections like the large private library of Joseph Toner and the riches of incunabula contained in the John Boyd Thacher collection were acquired by the Library of Congress, it became clear that the materials deserved a facility of their own. Thus the Rare Book Room (now the Rare Book and Special Collections Division) was established in 1927, and in

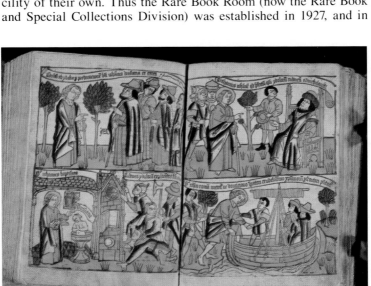

One of the treasures of the Lessing J. Rosenwald Collection is the block book, *Apocalypsis Sancti Johannis*

1934 the division moved into its present reading room and stack area, which were especially constructed (with extra attention given to the control of temperature and humidity) for the care and servicing of rare and unique materials.

An important point should be made here: the rare books and special collections in the Library of Congress are not just museum pieces, items for us to look at with awe and wonder through several layers of thick glass. Quite the contrary. They tell us a great deal about the history of printing, for example, or the development of the illustrated book, and even the evolution of that bestselling phenomenon, the cookbook. The treasures are here, it is true; and the superlatives are dramatic. The division's holdings of more than fifty-six hundred incunabula (books printed from the time of Gutenberg to 1501), for example, are the largest such collection in the Western Hemisphere. But, taken as a whole, the 300,000 volumes and the 200,000 broadsides, pamphlets, theater playbills, title pages, manuscripts, posters, and photographs are important because they form an essential part of this vast research library, this encyclopedia of knowledge we call the Library of Congress that today comprehends three different buildings.

Procedures for use. In common with other rare book facilities around the world, the Rare Book and Special Collections Division has some special procedures for the use of its materials. They are not meant to intimidate the reader, but rather are designed to provide a measure of security for its valuable materials.

If you wish to use some of the items in the Rare Book and Special Collections Reading Room, you will be asked to register at the reference desk inside the bronze doors, present proper identification, and check your coat, briefcase, and other packages at one of the lockers out in the hall. You will also be asked to take your notes with a pencil and not a ball-point or felt tip pen.

Once you have identified the specific items you want, calling on the reference staff for assistance if needed, you should fill out a request sheet for the desired items and take a seat at one of the tables in the reading room. The staff will deliver the materials to you. Resident specialists are also available to help you make the most efficient use of the division's collections in your subject area.

The collections. More than one-third of the volumes in the division's collections are shelved in order by Library of Congress classification number. The remaining two-thirds of the division's holdings have been organized into separately maintained collections. Some examples of these are: personal libraries (Thomas Jefferson, Woodrow Wilson, and Harry Houdini), comprehensive author collections (Walt Whitman, Sigmund Freud, and Hans Christian Andersen), subject collections (magic, gastronomy, and cryptography), the illustrated book (Rosenwald Collection), collections with unusual provenance (Russian Imperial and Third Reich Collections), and generic collections (miniature books, broadsides, dime novels, and Confederate States imprints). The division's collection of incunabula, as we mentioned, is unmatched on this side of the Atlantic; its Americana holdings constitute another overriding strength.

Catalogs and finding aids. The division has its own central card catalog, which contains 700,000 cards and provides access to almost all of its collections by author or other form of main entry. In addition, the division has created over one hundred special card files describing individual collections or special aspects of books from many collections. The latter file leads readers to materials via means not available in the regular catalogs—e.g., by date, place, and printer for books from the early years of printing. Other finding aids located in the division are printed catalogs that either describe individual collections or have been annotated to indicate the division's holdings.

Special services. The use of typewriters and voice recorders is permitted in the reading room as long as this does not disturb other readers. There are no photocopying machines in the reading room area, although in most cases photoreproductions can be ordered from the Library's Photoduplication Service.

GEOGRAPHY AND MAP READING ROOM

The Geography and Map Division of the Library of Congress has the largest and most comprehensive cartographic collection in the world. It contains 3,900,000 maps, 48,000 atlases, 2,000 three-dimensional plastic relief models, and a cartographic reference collection of over 8,000 volumes.

Its holdings start with a group of portolan atlases from the 1300s and 1400s (Italian, Spanish, and Portuguese of the Mediterranean area), proceed through rare manuscript maps from China from the 1600s, and come into our own time with maps by the millions. In any one year, the division will receive over fifty thousand new maps and eight hundred atlases.

Procedures for use. Of all the materials in the Library of Congress, there is no format that is as difficult to catalog, store, index, and handle as the great sheet maps of this division. For this reason, there is no simple access to the holdings. You should therefore go directly to the reference desk in the Geography and Map Reading Room and place your request with the specialist at the counter. The materials requested will be delivered promptly and laid out on wide tables in the Reading Room for your examination. Each section of the earth's surface has been mapped or charted for so many different reasons by so many different agencies, that the more clearly you can explain the purpose (as well as the place) that you are pursuing, the better the reference staff can serve you.

The collections. There are an astonishing number of *kinds* of maps available in the division's holdings. There are topographic, geologic, soil, mineral, and resources maps. The collections hold tens of thousands of maps of the bottom of the sea, census tracts, logging trails, the incidence of cancer, live mine fields, glacial moraines, annual income, and the back of the moon.

The historic maps of the division are frequently one-of-a-kind. The Faden Collection contains 101 maps of the French and Indian War and the American Revolution. The division also has several thousand maps of the American Civil War, many of which were used by army commanders in planning and executing their operations in the field. The Library has 700,000 large-scale Sanborn fire insurance maps which show commercial, industrial, and residential properties in 12,000 American cities since 1867. Many city blocks have been remapped as often as eight different times in the past one hundred years. (The material is heavily used by genealogists and social historians.)

All of the wars of the nineteenth and twentieth centuries are covered in great detail as mapped by each side in the conflicts, but the land use maps of the 1930s, the highway maps, and the official topographic maps (like our Geological Survey quadrangles or those produced by Britain's Ordnance Survey) from all the countries of the five continents equally fill the more than two acres of storage cases in the division.

Catalogs and finding aids. There is no comprehensive catalog of the Library's cartographic collections. There are, instead, many indexes and lists of special kinds of maps, such as the *Lowery Collection; A Descriptive List of Maps of the Spanish Possessions Within the Present Limits of the United States, 1502–1820.* And there are indexes of special publishers (the National Ocean Survey, and the British Ordnance Survey), and finding lists like the annual record of all maps deposited for copyright.

In 1969, for the first time, the Library's computerized cataloging programs made it possible to input cartographic descriptions and entries, and since that time, the division has gotten bibliographic con-

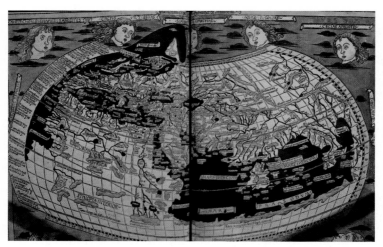

The world as it was perceived at the time of Columbus, depicted in *Cosmographia,* an atlas printed in Ulm, Germany, in 1482

trol over 250,000 individual sheets. The automated biliographic records may be accessed through terminals provided in the Geography and Map Reading Room.

Special services. Photoreproductions of maps and atlases not protected by copyright may be ordered from the Library's Photoduplication Service. In addition, there are light tables and drafting tables available in the Geography and Map Reading Room for the use of readers who wish to make tracings or drawings of maps.

The division has published an extensive number of bibliographies about portions of their collection through the years, so scholars can know not only what specific materials are in the Library, but can become aware of the kinds of information that maps can provide. A list of these publications is available, free, from the division. A sample of the titles includes: *Panoramic Maps of Cities in the United States and Canada, Railroad Maps of North America,* and an eight-volume *List of Geographical Atlases.*

HISPANIC READING ROOM

The Hispanic Reading Room is a dramatic tribute to Iberian and Latin American culture, with its Spanish Renaissance decor and furnishings, hammered silver brazier, Columbus coat of arms, and the four floor-to-ceiling murals by Brazilian artist Candido Portinari. The interest of the Library of Congress in the cultures and societies of Spanish and Portuguese speaking peoples, together with the support and encouragement of Archer M. Huntington (noted Hispanist and founder of the Hispanic Society of America), led to the creation of the Hispanic Division in 1939. The division continues to work to develop the Library's collections and to improve communications among scholars interested in Spanish, Portuguese, Caribbean, and Latin American affairs. Since its creation it has published guides, bibliographies, and studies to explain and facilitate the use of the Library's Spanish and Portuguese collections; some of these, like the *Handbook of Latin American Studies; A Selective and Annotated Guide to Recent Publications*, are among the basic research tools of the trade.

Procedures for use. If your primary focus is Latin American, Portuguese, or Spanish affairs, you will want to begin your research in the Hispanic Reading Room, even though some of the materials you may want to use will be located in other parts of the Library of Congress. Once you have registered, the reference librarian will describe the facilities of the reading room and provide assistance in the use of the reference collection and special finding aids available.

The collections. The approximately 1.9 million volumes in the Library's Hispanic collections are part of the general collections of the Library of Congress; they are not in the special custody of the Hispanic Division. Since the Library has long had a policy of acquiring complete sets of official gazettes, debates of parliamentary bodies, and all other significant official publications of national agencies as well as selected provincial or state imprints, its collection of official Latin American documents is among the strongest in the world. Similarly, it has an outstanding collection of Hispanic newspapers. Important groups of Hispanic materials can also be found in the Manuscript, Rare Book and Special Collections, Music, Prints and Photographs, and Geography and Map Divisions, as well as the Law Library.

The most significant single collection in the custody of the Hispanic Division is the Archive of Hispanic Literature on Tape. The Archive was started in 1942 to capture original voice recordings of selections of the writings of contemporary Iberian, Caribbean, and Latin American poets and prose writers. The Archive now contains some six hundred authors, whose voices researchers may listen to in an alcove of the reading room. A complete catalog of the tapes, as well as the written texts of the recorded works, are available for reference purposes. A 3,500-volume reference collection, a pamphlet and technical report collection, vertical files accessible by subject, and newspaper clippings from information services on Latin America are some of the other resources readers will find to assist them in the Hispanic Reading Room.

Catalogs and finding aids. Copies of the published guides to certain portions of the Library's Hispanic collections, many of them prepared in cooperation with other scholarly associations, are located in the Hispanic Reading Room, and they constitute a major source of information about what you can expect to find in the collections. *Human Rights in Latin America: A Bibliography, Cuban Acquisitions and Bibliography,* and *The Hans P. Kraus Collection of Hispanic American Manuscripts; A Guide* are some examples. *The Handbook of Latin American Studies,* published since 1936, is the basic reference and acquisition tool for that area. The staff that prepares the *Handbook* are also located in the Hispanic Division and constitute a useful informa-

"The Mining of Gold," one of a series of four murals in the Hispanic Reading Room by Brazilian artist Candido Portinari

tion source for data on the latest publications on Latin America. You will also find in the reading room reference guides to other Hispanic collections around the country, guides to the Hispanic manuscripts in the custody of the Library's Manuscript Division, and a guide to over eight thousand Spanish plays. Many of these resources are unique to the Library of Congress in the Washington, D.C., area. Finally, a terminal to tap into the Library's Computerized Catalog is available for reader use.

Special services.   Since one of the original purposes of the Hispanic Division was to facilitate communications and the cross fertilization of research among scholars working in Hispanic, Portuguese, and Latin American studies, it is not surprising that the Hispanic Division tries to assist researchers by relating the Library's collections to other sources of Hispanic materials, both in Washington and around the country. The division's reference librarians will often go to considerable effort to help the researcher make use of all the relevant collections he may need, wherever they happen to be located.

Special study facilities in the reading room alcoves are available to scholars who expect to be doing research at the Library of Congress over an extended period of time, and typewriters and voice recorders may be used in those facilities. Two microform readers are available for readers to make use of relevant microform materials from other collections in the Library. Exhibit cases in the entrance halls to the Hispanic Reading Room display items of interest from the Hispanic collections.

EUROPEAN READING ROOM

If you are a reader whose study relates to the European countries (excluding Spain, Portugal, and the British Isles), you should begin your research in the European Reading Room. Because relevant books are dispersed throughout the general collections, however, you will undoubtedly need to pursue your subject in the general reading rooms as well. In addition, the European Law, Geography and Map, Music, Prints and Photographs, Rare Book and Special Collections, and Manuscript Divisions have important collections of Slavic and European materials that should not be overlooked.

The acquisition in 1906 of an 80,000-volume collection of books and periodicals, most of them in Russian, from a Siberian merchant and bibliophile named G. V. Yudin, was the impetus for collecting Slavic materials in the Library of Congress. Yudin had developed one of the finest personal libraries in the Russian Empire, and his collection contained many eighteenth-century works and long runs of periodicals and government publications. Lenin himself used Yudin's library when he was exiled to Siberia from 1897 to 1898. The collection is especially rich in Siberian materials, gathered from Yudin's native region. Although many of these materials are now dispersed throughout the Library of Congress, they are available for researchers to draw upon. Interest in the Slavic countries following the Second World War led to the creation of a Slavic Division in the Library of Congress in 1951. It has evolved in recent years into the European Division.

Procedures for use. The European Reading Room is staffed by multilingual reference librarians who can direct you to the materials you may need and answer reference questions on the collections in their custody. Area specialists are available to respond to the more complex queries that require indepth knowledge of a country's history or culture.

The collections. The European Reading Room contains a reference collection of about ten thousand volumes on Europe (excluding Spain, Portugal, and the British Isles), with special strength in Russia and the Soviet Union. It also has custody of current, unbound Slavic and Baltic periodicals (about 8,500 titles, including 250 newspapers) as well as several special collections of older monographs, serials, and pamphlets dating from 1880 to 1940. The Library's overall holdings in European materials are especially strong in history, language, literature, economics, government and politics, geography, and law. Extra attention has been devoted to the collections in science and technology since 1950.

Catalogs and finding aids. The Library's general catalogs provide access to many of the Slavic and other European materials in the collections. In addition, the Cyrillic Union Catalog (containing bibliographic information on Cyrillic alphabet publications with pre-1956 imprints) and the Slavic Cyrillic Union Catalog which supplements it, are available both in the Main Reading Room and in the European Reading Room (in microform). Books in the Cyrillic alphabet have been included in the Library of Congress Computerized Catalog since 1979. Specialized guides to the collections are prepared by the staff of the division and are available in the reading room. One of these, *The American Bibliography of Slavic and East European Studies,* is an annual publication published in cooperation with the American Association for the Advancement of Slavic Studies. It cites books, periodical articles, published reports, and scholarly book reviews by American and Canadian authors on Slavic and East European subjects in the social sciences and the humanities, and it has become one of the major research tools in the field.

Special services.   The professional area specialists and reference staff of the European Division are prepared to give special assistance to scholars in locating the research materials they need in the Library of Congress.

ASIAN READING ROOM

The oldest—and some of the most glorious—treasures of the Library of Congress are in the custody of the Asian Division: early block-printed books, pictographic manuscripts from a tribe in southwestern China, books printed with movable wooden type long before Gutenberg's day, brilliantly hand-illuminated manuscript volumes created in the seventeenth century, a scroll sutra from 975, and an ancient example of Japanese printing dating from 770. They are beautiful and rare examples of Oriental culture and art. But the real strength of the Asian Division is its rich research collections of books, periodicals, newspapers, manuscripts, and microform materials in more than twenty Asian languages. These are the collections you will need to draw on if you are a student of Chinese, Japanese, Korean, or South and Southeast Asian culture and society.

Procedures for use.   To begin your research in the Asian Division, first visit the section (Chinese and Korean, Japanese, or Southern Asian) that covers your subject area. The Southern Asian Section includes India, Pakistan, Sri Lanka, Bangladesh, Nepal, Burma, Thailand, Laos, Cambodia, Vietnam, Singapore, Malaysia, Brunei, Indonesia, and the Philippines. Consult with the reference librarians in the various sections, locate the items you want in the card catalogs, and fill out call slips to request the materials. The staff will retrieve the books from the division's collections and bring them to you in the Asian Reading Room. Books and periodicals concerning these countries that are published in western languages are part of the Library's general collections and accessible through one of the general reading rooms.

The collections.   The Chinese collections, the largest in the West, include some five hundred thousand volumes in the Chinese language, as well as several thousand in the Manchu, Mongol, Tibetan, and Mo-so languages. They got their start with an exchange of ten Chinese titles in 933 volumes from the Emperor of China in 1869. The Asian Division now receives current Chinese publications from the People's Republic of China, Taiwan, and Hong Kong on a regular basis through purchases from designated blanket order dealers and through official exchange agreements. The Chinese holdings also include periodicals and newspapers, as well as some ten thousand reels of microfilm that supplement the printed materials. The Chinese collections are particularly rich in local histories, traditional Chinese series *(ts'ung shu),* and collected works of individual authors. Most of the Korean collections have come to the Library since 1950 when that unit was created. They now consist of more than seventy-six thousand volumes and thirty-two hundred serial titles. A special effort is being made to strengthen the Library's holdings of North Korean publications. The Japanese language collection of almost seven hundred thousand volumes constitutes the largest such resource outside of Japan. Indeed, many of the titles cannot be found inside Japan itself. The Library's holdings are especially strong in the humanities and social sciences of Japan, Taiwan, Korea, and Manchuria, and in scientific and technological serials. The selected archives of the Japanese Foreign Office, Army, Navy and other government agencies from 1868 to 1945 are contained on more than two thousand four hundred reels of microfilm. Together, the Chinese, Japanese, and Korean collections make up 80 to 90 percent of the division's holdings. The Library's Southern Asian materials are estimated at four hundred and fifty thousand volumes, one hundred and eighty thousand of which are in the languages of the region and serviced by the Asian Division. The section also maintains a collection of more than three thousand current newspaper and periodical titles.

This is a Chinese version of the *Lotus Sutra* printed from blocks on a scroll 68 feet long and 6½ inches wide, c. 1050.

115

Catalogs and finding aids. The division has extensive card catalogs for the collections within its custody. Union catalogs of Chinese and Japanese materials in other libraries are also available. In addition, specialized finding aids and bibliographies have been prepared by the various sections to assist readers in their use of the collections.

Special services. Microform and microfiche readers are accessible for use by readers. Scholars doing extended research may place materials they are working with on reserve in the reading room. If researchers have been assigned special study facilities by the Research Facilities Office, they may use materials from the Asian Division, together with books from the general collections, at these facilities.

AFRICAN AND MIDDLE EASTERN DIVISION

The African and Middle Eastern Division consists of three sections which provide reference and research services on the Library's collections for the countries of the African continent and the Middle East: the African Section, the Hebraic Section, and the Near East Section. Each section can accommodate a small number of researchers, but there is no common reading room. For the sake of simplicity, these sections will be treated here as a unit, and a separate discussion of their individual collections and reader facilities is provided.

The *Washington Haggadah* is an illuminated Hebrew manuscript executed in Germany or North Italy in 1478.

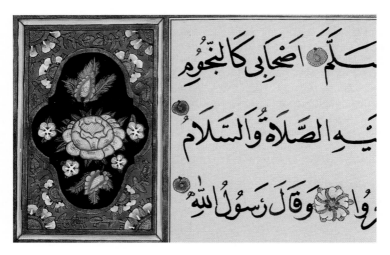

An example
of Arabic cal-
ligraphy from
the Near
East Section

Procedures for use.   Reference specialists in the three sections
will help to acquaint you with the resources available in the Library.
Many materials, especially those relating to sub-Saharan Africa, are
part of the general book and periodical collections. The staff will
also guide you in the use of the reference works and specialized files
maintained by the section.

The collections.   The African Section provides a focal point for
the Library's reference and bibliographic activities related to the
countries of sub-Saharan Africa (excluding the North African nations of Algeria, Egypt, Libya, Morocco, and Tunisia). The Library's
holdings in Africana, dispersed throughout the general collections,
are especially strong in the areas of economics, history, linguistics,
and literature. The section maintains a small reference collection of
bibliographies, yearbooks, and unpublished research papers, as well
as a growing pamphlet collection. The Hebraic Section has custody of
more than one hundred and twenty thousand volumes and of extensive microform holdings in Hebrew, Yiddish, Aramaic, Syriac, Ethi-
opic, and cognate languages, with the great preponderance in Hebrew
and Yiddish. These cover such topics as the Bible, the cultures and
languages of the ancient Near East, Jews and Judaism throughout the
world from Biblical times to the present, Palestine and Israel, and
Ethiopia. Books in Western languages on these topics are shelved
with the Library's general collections, with a selection of major refer-

ence works in the Hebraic Section office. The section also maintains a collection of current periodicals and newspapers in the relevant languages. Materials in Arabic, Turkish, Persian, Armenian, and other languages of the Middle East (excluding Hebrew) are under the jurisdiction of the Near East Section. Arabic works dominate their collection of more than one hundred and thirty thousand volumes, which has especially good coverage of area languages and linguistic science; ancient, medieval, and modern history; the vernacular press; and government publications.

Catalogs and finding aids. The African Section compiles a number of guides to Africana material as aids to researchers. These cover various kinds of publications, such as periodical literature and government documents, and include topical studies on such subjects as petroleum resources and international relations. Card indexes to monographs and periodicals are also available in the section. The Hebraic Section maintains union catalogs of Hebraica and Yiddica in major collections of the United States and Canada. The bibliographic program of the Near East Section includes the preparation of guides to a wide range of topics, such as American doctoral dissertations on the Arab world and Turkish political developments, plus the maintenance of union catalogs to material within its area of concern and special indexes to items in its own collections.

Special services. Area specialists are available to the serious scholar to assist with his study of the countries and cultures covered by this division. The specialists will also help to direct the researcher to materials and collections in other locations (both inside and outside the Library of Congress) that might be useful.

Index Italicized page numbers indicate primary descriptive passages.

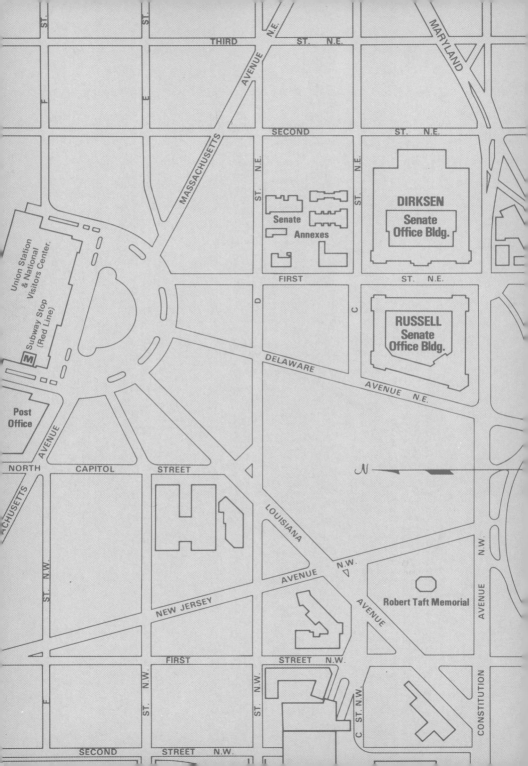